TITCH

A HISTORY

Abbey Tile

In spite of the great wealth of available material, no one before has attempted to write anything larger than a slim parish guide about Titchfield. The members of the Titchfield History Society who prepared this present volume are well aware that it is not a piece of professional historical writing. It is an attempt to introduce a wider public to the main themes in the history of the village, and to guide those who would like to enquire further. The authors would like to thank all those who have answered questions, supplied information and undertaken tedious chores during the preparation of this volume. They dedicate it to everyone who has ever lived in Titchfield, past and present.

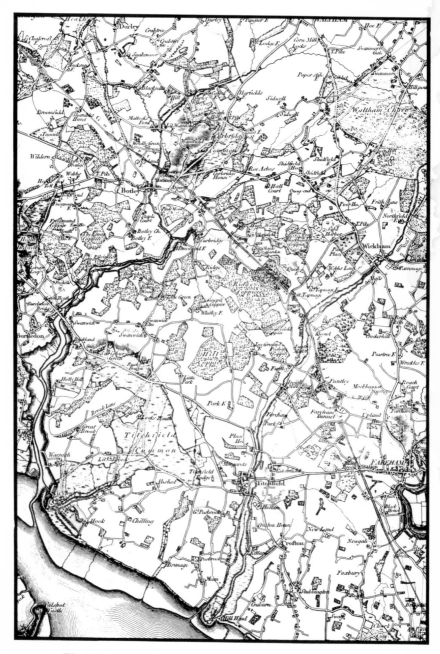

Titchfield and district in the early nineteenth century

2

TITCHFIELD

———— A HISTORY ————

Contributors:
Christine Bartlett, Vernon Belding, Tony Clare,
Trevor Cox, Keith Dingle, Christopher Draper,
Gwen Edwards, Michael Hare, Alice James,
Ian Jameson, Andrew King, Simon Matthews,
Philip Silvester, Peter Singer, Richard Wade,
George Watts, Sally Wise

Maps and drawings: Vernon Belding

Edited by George Watts for the
Titchfield History Society

Jutish brooch

Designed and Printed by Polygraphic Limited, Titchfield

Contents

Introduction

The village

Few English villages or small towns have as rich and varied a history as Titchfield. We hope in this small book to introduce the interested reader to some of its riches, and to show him or her where there are yet more things to be discovered. In Titchfield there are important palaeolithic remains; the oldest standing piece of ecclesiastical architecture in Hampshire; the site of a famous monastic library; a handsome late medieval barn; buildings associated with our

Abbey tile

greatest dramatist; one of the earliest of English canals; and the remains of one of the best known industrial developments of the eighteenth century. Here rested Henry V before Agincourt and Charles I before his imprisonment at Carisbrooke. And in our own century, in spite of the suburbanisation creeping over the hillsides to east and west, the village and its people have retained the quirky, robust individuality which once made them less than respectful tenants of their medieval landlord - an individuality which may seem puzzling in a community almost sandwiched between two great modern cities. This history may go some way towards explaining that distinctive village character: so too will a stroll around its streets and its lanes.

The land

The tract of countryside in which Titchfield grew up is in that part of Hampshire to the south of the chalk downs, a gently rolling low plateau of clay and gravel deeply cut by its rivers and small streams. This territory lay on both sides of the river Meon, stretching towards the river Hamble on the west and towards the Wallington and Fareham creek on the east. The attractive modern coastline came into existence only in mesolithic times when the sea flooded the valley of the prehistoric Solent river. Thereafter, until 1611, the Meon was a salt-water estuary, the very highest tides creeping up to the floors of cottages in the village Square.

In early times only tiny groups of people wandered across this district, hunting, fishing and collecting wild plants. Much of the land was heavily wooded: the great area of woodland in the Middle Ages called the Forest of Bere lay right across the north of the parish. On the more badly drained and poorer soils the ancient woodland survives to this day on land which has never been cultivated, though it has been heavily cut over during coppicing and charcoal burning. Further to the south, large areas of land, when cleared by the early farmers, revealed better soils which are still producing good crops today. Some of the poorer though well-drained soils remained as common and heathland until the nineteenth century, but then, by a profitable coincidence and in combination with a mild climate, proved to be very suitable to the newly introduced strawberries, for which Hampshire became famous in the fruit markets of London. Farming, market gardening and greenhouse cultivation continue to play an important part in the life of the parish; less prominent than in earlier times are livestock - the goats from which the village probably took its name, the pigs which wandered through the medieval forest and the great herds of sheep which were a feature of the district until the early 1800's. But Titchfield has never been an entirely agricultural community. From very early times it had markets and fairs, and developed into a town of fair size by medieval standards. Within it, tanning, milling, brewing, weaving and many other activities offered varied employment to its inhabitants for several centuries, while in recent times modern industrial and commercial concerns have found a home here. Unlike some communities, Titchfield has become neither a dormitory suburb nor an excessively preserved residential backwater: it remains a place in which history is something which is happening now, and not yet something which has happened only in the past.

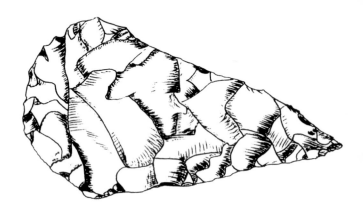

Acheulian Axe

The Earliest Men

Long before the sea flooded the valley of the Solent river and created the modern coastline, primitive hunters wandered across the land later to be called Titchfield. Hundreds of flint tools, and thousands of flint flakes, left by the very primitive palaeolithic (Old Stone Age) people of more than 500,000 years ago called by archaeologists "Clactonian", have been found on Rainbow Bar, the spit off Meon beach which is exposed at low tide (map reference SU531021). Other flint hand-axes of a later phase of the Old Stone Age, the "Acheulian" period, have been found near Hook and in the gravel cliff face which runs behind the beach from Meon westwards to Chilling.

After the last Ice Age when the coast and valleys were taking on their modern shape, in the period we call the Middle Stone Age or "Mesolithic", small groups of people moved along the coasts, hunting, fishing, collecting shells and nuts, and they too have left evidence in the form of flint axes, scrapers and flint arrowheads scattered through the parish. In the New Stone Age, the "Neolithic", perhaps 3000 B.C., when agriculture was first practised, there may for a time have been a settlement in the area, for two important finds - an imported black jade axe and a flint sickle - were made during earth removal at the gravel pit between Meon hamlet and the river.

In the Bronze Age, about 1500 B.C., when Salisbury Plain and the Hampshire Downs were settled by the people who used Stonehenge and other great monuments, the coastal lowlands of Hampshire seem to have been largely neglected, used only as pathways to the interior. The finds of this period in Titchfield suggest the temporary camps of travellers rather than settlements. The single spearhead and seven bronze axe-heads of the type called palstaves found in 1880 and handed to the vicar were probably the buried hoard of a bronze-smith. Another palstave of a type found in Brittany has been picked up in a strawberry field at Meonbye Farm. Along the Hamble near Swanwick, a pit of this period unearthed in the 1940's contained two burial urns, bones and evidence of burning, which suggested some kind of religious ceremony. But it is not until the last centuries B.C. that we have clear evidence, discussed below, of a settlement of a permanent kind, and then only on a small scale.

Palstave

7

Britons and Romans

The people we come to know in history as the Britons entered Britain during the Iron Age, but in the Titchfield area evidence for settlement in the later Iron Age is limited to a single partially excavated site and a few chance finds. A site just north of the hamlet of Hook (SU511054), which was revealed by gravel excavations and partly excavated in 1954, provided evidence of occupation in the late Bronze Age, the late Iron Age and continuing into the Roman period. In the late Iron Age the bank of an earlier banked and ditched enclosure had been razed and a palisade erected on the line of the infilled ditch. The trenches into which the palisade had been set yielded late Iron Age pottery and cut through deposits containing similar pottery, demonstrating several phases of activity on the site in the late Iron Age. This scanty evidence suggests that this was an enclosed settlement site, which may have been defended. Other evidence possibly relating to settlements of this period comes in the form of finds of pottery from Cumber Copse, south of Sarisbury (SU5037073), and Chark Common (SU570160), and a gold coin of the British leader Tricomminus, now in the British Museum, found on the hill opposite the church.

Apart from settlements there is also evidence of salt working in this period from two sites on the coast. The first of these is a beach site below Hook Bungalow (SU503040) where pottery and briquetage were found in association with areas of burnt clay. The second is a cliff top site at Brownwich Farm (SU520032). Excavations here in 1971 revealed a gulley, in the bottom of which were two burnt hearth or oven areas containing daub, pottery, briquetage and burnt flint. There was also evidence of a semi-circular windbreak against the prevailing south westerly winds, and a hard packed clay floor area. Briquetage is a coarse, ceramic material used in salt production, and its presence, together with the absence of domestic refuse, indicates the industrial nature of these two sites. Salt has always been a valuable commodity, and its commercial importance in the later Iron Age is being increasingly recognised by historians. These sites in the Titchfield area are only two of a large number on the south and east coasts from Dorset to Lincolnshire.

Evidence from elsewhere in southern England suggests that, in general, rural settlement was not markedly disrupted by the Roman conquest of Britain following the invasion of 43 A.D. However, within the Titchfield area such evidence is confined to the site near Hook, where there is a rectilinear enclosure of the Roman period just to the east of the late Iron Age occupation already mentioned.

Romano-British activity is in evidence at four other sites within the parish. A pit containing Romano-British pottery was discovered near Woodside Farm just north of the motorway (SU535084), and a timber-framed well, found during clay extraction near Swanwick (SU503100), produced Samian and coarse wares. Sherds of Romano-British pottery have been found in the Warsash area, and during the construction of a golf course on Chark Common the remains of what is believed to be a Roman pottery kiln was discovered.

There are no known Roman roads within the ancient parish boundary of Titchfield, but two roads skirt the parish on the north and east. The archaeologist I.D. Margary has given Roman roads numbers for easier identification; the road between Chichester and Bitterne is route 421 and that between Winchester and Wickham 420. It is unfortunate that it is precisely in the area around Titchfield that the lines of these roads are least known. To the west, route 421 is well attested from Bitterne as far as Botley, and to the east from Wickham to Chichester. Route 420 from Winchester is known as far as Cold Harbour, near Wickham, and there is a short stretch of road known to be south of Wickham, which appears to be heading towards Fareham, possibly with Portchester as its ultimate destination.

There is no evidence for a Roman origin for Titchfield itself; the major settlement nuclei in the Roman period appear to have been at Fareham and Wickham. Fareham is situated in a good position on high ground overlooking the Wallington estuary, with views to the east and south. In Roman times there was probably a silt-free channel into Portsmouth harbour. Information from small excavations and chance finds makes it certain that there was activity in the area in the first and second centuries A.D. and Fareham may have been a port as early as the late first century. A small excavation on the site of the Crown Offices produced pottery of late first to fourth century date, associated with a ditch and evidence of structures. The excavation suggested the possibility of economic growth and population expansion after the end of the third century as a response to the new military market at Portchester, which was established as a "Saxon Shore" fort at that time.

At Wickham, the meeting of routes 420 and 421, the crossing of 421 over the River Meon and quantities of occupation debris all indicate the existence of some kind of minor urban settlement, probably a "mansio" or road station. Finds of pottery suggest a date for the establishment of the settlement within ten or fifteen years of the invasion of 43 A.D. and the distribution of finds suggests that it may have been fairly extensive, although no structural evidence has yet come to light.

9

Further west, near Curbridge, at the point where route 421 crosses the navigable River Hamble, just south of Fairthorne (SU520118), structural remains have been found. These represent a large building or a complex of smaller ones, which, on the evidence of the pottery, was occupied from the late first to late fourth centuries. Between Wickham and the Fairthorne site were first century A.D. pottery kilns in Hallcourt Wood near Shedfield and also brick and tile kiln sites south of Fairthorne Grange.

The evidence we have at present for the Roman period suggests therefore that the Romans and their British subjects sailed up the Hamble to Fairthorne, making some use of the Hook and Swanwick areas, and up the creek to Fareham, and then travelled inland by their two roads. Although "Meon" is a word of British or Celtic origin, they seem to have made little if any use of this river, and we must assume that the site of Titchfield and most of the later parish was in those days covered by marsh, forest or trackless heath.

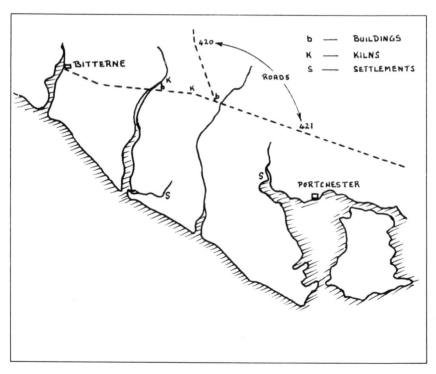

Roman Sites

Saxons and Jutes

It is in the Anglo-Saxon period that Titchfield first appears as a settlement, though the origin of the town is obscure. In the post-Roman period much of eastern and southern England was settled by Anglo-Saxon invaders. But Meon is an ancient British word, and it was from the river that the settlers in our area took their name, calling themselves the Meonware. The Venerable Bede, writing in the year 732, describes how England was

Jutish Brooch

settled by Angles, Saxons and Jutes. The Jutes settled in Kent, the Isle of Wight and in the Meon valley. The Meonware were, therefore, distinct from the main body of settlers in central southern England, the West Saxons; they retained a separate identity at least until the late seventh century.

Evidence from the pagan period is slender, but an important cemetery of sixth century date was found at Droxford during the construction of the Meon Valley railway in 1900 and has recently been re-excavated. Nothing of this period has been found in the immediate vicinity of Titchfield, but there is an interesting reference in the tenth century to a feature near Segensworth called *tidiceshlaewe*, Tidic's barrow. Tidic might have been an important early leader of the Meonware, and it is possible that Tidic's barrow was an important burial, perhaps comparable to those excavated at Sutton Hoo and at Taplow (originally *taeppeshlaewe)*. Unfortunately no trace of the barrow can now be found.

In the second half of the seventh century the Meonware were involved in territorial disputes, and we know something of the history of this small kingdom at this time. In the middle of the seventh century the two kingdoms of Mercia and Wessex were striving for supremacy. In 661 King Wulfhere of Mercia defeated the West Saxons in battle, and subsequently gave the territory of the Meonware to his ally, King Aethelwealh of Sussex. As far as we know, Aethelwealh retained the Meon valley in his possession until his death. This seems to have taken place in 685 at the hands of Caedwalla, an exiled prince of the royal house of Wessex, who ruled only from 686 to 688, when he abdicated and went to Rome. It seems likely that it was at this time that the territory of the Meonware was absorbed into the kingdom of Wessex. The consolidation of the power of Wessex was continued by Caedwalla's successor, King Ine (688-726); during his reign Wessex was the dominant power in southern England.

11

It was in the course of the seventh century that the Meonware were converted to Christianity. A church was founded at Winchester in about 648 and it is possible that the conversion of the Meonware ensued shortly thereafter. It is, however, more probable that the Meonware remained pagan for another generation, like their neighbours the South Saxons and the inhabitants of the Isle of Wight. The conversion of Sussex took place after 681, when King Aethelwealh invited the great Northumbrian prelate St. Wilfred to undertake a mission in his kingdom. As we have already seen, the Meon valley was apparently under Aethelwealh's control at this time, so it is more than likely that the Meonware were converted along with the South Saxons.

Wilfrid's influence in the area did not come to an end when Caedwalla killed Aethelwealh in 685. In 686 the Isle of Wight was evangelised by disciples of Wilfrid, after a merciless conquest by Caedwalla, and Bede comments that the Isle of Wight was the last of the kingdoms of Britain to receive the faith of Christ. We can, therefore, be certain that by 686 the Meonware were at least nominally Christian.

It is not improbable that Titchfield played an important role in the events of these years. It is of particular interest to note that the church was probably built in the late seventh century or in the early eighth century and that the building is comparable to the churches of that date in Northumbria. In view of the presence of Wilfrid in the area, it is probable that the church was built by him or at least under his influence in the succeeding generation. In the writer's own personal view, the most likely patron is Caedwalla during his short reign from 686 to 688. We know the close links between Wilfrid and Caedwalla, and we also know that the conquest of the Isle of Wight was followed closely by the introduction of Christianity. Is it not equally possible that Caedwalla built churches in the Meon Valley as part of a policy of pacification of the area after his succession to the kingdom of Wessex in 686?

From its origins Titchfield was a minster church, that is to say a church staffed by a small body of clergy responsible for the pastoral care of a wide area. Titchfield appears to have been responsible for a vast area of the lower Meon valley. Its original parish seems to have stretched from the Hamble River in the west to Portsmouth Harbour in the east; it extended from the shore of the Solent in the south to Wickham and the Forest of Bere in the north. The upper reaches of the Meon Valley were probably served by another minster church at East Meon, while a further minster church existed at Bishops Waltham.

Minster churches were usually found on royal estates, and it seems probable that in the late seventh century the area served by the minster church of Titchfield corresponded to a large royal estate. Titchfield itself

12

remained in royal hands until after the Norman Conquest, though other parts of the estate were granted away by the Kings of Wessex.

It should be stressed that although we know from architectural evidence that an important church existed at Titchfield from an early date, we have no written records which refer to Titchfield at this time. After the late seventh century we know little of Titchfield itself or of the Meonware, who seem to have been absorbed peacefully into the kingdom of Wessex.

To summarise, it seems most probable that Titchfield began life as the centre of a large royal estate and that in the late seventh century an important church was constructed. We do, however, know nothing about the development of this settlement into a small medieval town. Archaeological observation on a number of sites has failed so far to produce any evidence from the Anglo-Saxon period.

What we do know is that the church continued to serve as a minster church at least into the tenth century. Life cannot always have been peaceful for the clergy of the minster. Several raids by Vikings on the south coast of Hampshire are recorded in the second half of the ninth century and during the renewed invasions of the late tenth and early eleventh century the Viking army wintered several times on the Isle of Wight. The Isle of Wight is clearly visible from the roof of Titchfield Church, and the substantial Anglo-Saxon Church must equally have been a tempting target for the Vikings. It may, however, be noted that although Titchfield was probably plundered on several occasions, the early Church shows no traces of burning.

The earliest documentary reference to Titchfield occurs in a Charter of King Ethelred the Unready of the year 982. This refers to an earlier transaction that had taken place in the reign of King Eadred (946-955), in which a certain Lufa acquired six small estates, four in the Isle of Wight, one on Portsea Island and one near Titchfield at Segensworth. Subsequently they were purchased by the earldorman (nobleman) Aethelmaer, who, in his will, left this land to the New Minster at Winchester. The six estates are not specified by name in Aethelmaer's will, but fortunately King Ethelred confirmed the estates in a Charter which describes the boundaries of each estate.

Titchfield is mentioned twice in this charter. The lands included an estate at a place called Stathe, in the Isle of Wight; its exact location is now lost but it was probably on the north coast opposite the mouth of the Meon. One section of the boundaries of Stathe reads "to the boundary of the members of the community of Titchfield". In other words the religious community at Titchfield owned land on the Isle of Wight immediately adjacent to the estate at Stathe. In this connection it is worth noting that when Caedwalla conquered the Isle of Wight in 686, he gave a quarter of the island to Wilfrid. It has already been suggested that Wilfrid may have founded Titchfield Church; is it possible that the land held by Titchfield in the tenth century is a remnant of this gift made in the seventh century? Unfortunately no later references to this land can be traced.

The second reference in Ethelred's charter states that the members of the community at Titchfield had been witnesses to the original charter granted by King Eadred to Lufa. We do therefore have clear evidence of the continuing existence of a religious community at Titchfield in the tenth century. It was, however, probably already in decline. In the late-Saxon period the large minster parishes began to break up to form smaller parishes.

The concept of a church in each village began to take shape. Fareham and Alverstoke both belonged to the Bishop of Winchester and probably had their own parish churches by the tenth century. Rowner was probably also a separate parish by the time of the Norman Conquest, while Wickham obtained independent parochial rights in the twelfth century. The ancient mother church of Titchfield remained a large parish, but from the eleventh century onwards it was probably served only by a single priest.

After 982 our next reference to Titchfield is found in the Domesday Survey of 1086. By this time it was clearly a substantial settlement with its own market. However at present we can only guess as to how and why the settlement grew to its Domesday size.

We may conclude this section by some thoughts on the origin of the place-name Titchfield. In its first appearance, in the charter of 982, it appears as *ticcefelda*. The second element, *feld*, simply denotes open land, but the first element is open to speculation. Most authorities consider that it comes from the Anglo-Saxon word *ticce*, "a kid", and that the original meaning of Titchfield was thus the "open land where goats were pastured". It is however possible that the first element in fact derived from an otherwise unrecorded personal name Ticce. It is worth noting that the same elements occur in the earliest forms of other south-east Hampshire place-names, such as Tisted and Tichborne. Our hypothetical Ticce could therefore be an important early settler, with interests over a wide area. In this connection it is worth looking again at the occurence of "Tidic's barrow" near Segensworth. It is no more than speculation, but it is just possible that Ticce and Tidic were both early members of the royal family of the Meonware. Titchfield, at all events, remained a royal estate. The mill was called the King's Mill, and the estate was in the hands of Edward the Confessor before the Norman Conquest.

14

The Parish Church

Only a brief account of Titchfield church is given in this history. A detailed guide-book may be purchased in the church and there is a display area inside the church devoted to its history and architecture.

St. Peter's Keys

In the previous chapter of this History attention was drawn to the status of Titchfield church as an early minster. The surviving remains of the Anglo-Saxon period reflect this status. The west wall of the aisleless Anglo-Saxon nave, together with a west porch, are preserved almost intact in the existing building. The porch now forms the lower part of the west tower and retains the original entrance arch. To the south of the tower the south-west corner of the Anglo-Saxon nave can be seen, preserved to its full height of almost 30ft. The length of the original nave is uncertain, but is likely to have been the same as the present nave; nothing is known of the Anglo-Saxon chancel though it was undoubtedly much shorter than the present chancel. Recent study has shown that the surviving Anglo-Saxon fabric is probably to be dated to the earliest days of Christianity in the area, the late seventh or early eighth century. There are close parallels between Titchfield and the early churches of Northumbria, the home territory of St. Wilfred.

In the later Middle Ages, the Anglo-Saxon church was gradually enlarged, reflecting the increasing prosperity of the settlement, and, from the thirteenth century, the stimulus provided by the foundation of Titchfield Abbey. The first alterations were made in the twelfth century. A south aisle was added to the nave (subsequently pulled down in the nineteenth century); at the same time the elaborate carved doorway opening from the tower into the nave was inserted in place of the original Anglo-Saxon doorway. At the end of the twelfth or in the early thirteenth century the Anglo-Saxon porch was raised to form the present tower. In the thirteenth century an extended chancel was built, and in the first half of the fourteenth century, a chapel was added on its south side.

Several changes may be ascribed to the fifteenth century. The chancel was extensively remodelled and a north aisle was added. This aisle, with its tall slender columns and large traceried windows, is of particularly fine design. It also seems probable that it was during the fifteenth century that a spire was added to the tower.

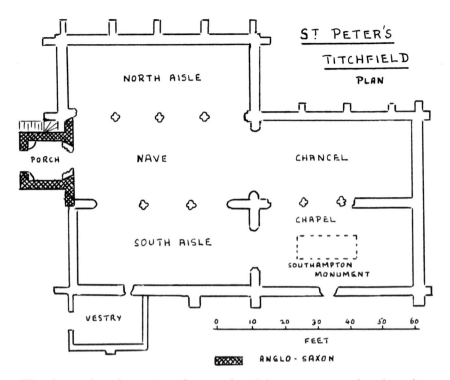

ST PETER'S

TITCHFIELD

PLAN

NORTH AISLE

PORCH

NAVE

CHANCEL

CHAPEL

SOUTH AISLE

SOUTHAMPTON
MONUMENT

VESTRY

0 10 20 30 40 50 60

FEET

ANGLO - SAXON

The sixteenth and seventeenth centuries did not see any major alterations to the fabric of the church, but the Reformation led to drastic changes in its internal appearance. The medieval stained glass windows were destroyed, the mural paintings whitewashed over, the elaborate screens which sub-divided the church removed and all the other trappings of medieval finery swept away. In its place an interior altogether more austere in character emerged. The appearance of the church in the Georgian period can be judged from a water-colour painting in the display area in the church. A three-decker pulpit dominates the nave which is filled with box pews. These pews were reserved almost entirely for the middle and upper classes, and in due course it became necessary to add galleries at the west end and on the south side to provide additional accommodation.

In the nineteenth century further changes in attitude and fashion took place, which resulted in a major restoration in 1866-7. The box-pews and galleries were anathema to the Victorians and were removed; they were replaced by the present plain pews which were open to parishioners of every social class. Sadly the restoration also involved the destruction of the Norman south aisle and its replacement by a much larger aisle in the Decorated style.

St. Peter's Church

Since 1866-7 the only structural change has been the addition of a vestry at the south-west corner of the church in 1905. However by the end of the Second World War it had become clear that the structure of the building was in very poor condition throughout. The last thirty years have seen a steady programme of restoration initiated by the Reverend Norman Miller, vicar from 1947 to 1973. Much work still needs to be done.

It remains to comment briefly on the monuments in Titchfield church, which range from the thirteenth century to the present day. The earliest monument is a much worn effigy of a knight in armour, dateable on stylistic grounds to the end of the thirteenth century. It is to be seen at the east end of the chapel on the south side of the chancel. Pride of place among the monuments must necessarily go to the massive Southampton Monument, which dominates the same chapel. The Earls of Southampton and their place in the history of Titchfield are discussed elsewhere. The monument was erected under the terms of the will of the second Earl of Southampton and commemorates himself and his father and mother, the first Earl and Countess. It is among the finest surviving Elizabethan monuments and was erected about 1594 by one of the best known sculptors of the period, Gerard Johnson, a Flemish refugee. The detail on the three effigies is particularly noteworthy.

From the early seventeenth century onwards monuments survive from almost every generation. Many of them commemorate figures prominent in the history of Titchfield, but they are too numerous to be discussed individually. It will be seen that a good number of monuments are to naval officers, colonial governors, soldiers and the like; with its proximity to Portsmouth, Titchfield has always been an attractive place of residence for members of the services and their families.

What *is* Titchfield?

As a known locality, Titchfield seems to have begun its existence as a small kingdom or sub-tribal territory of the Meonware. After its conquest by the West Saxon kings it has been suggested that it became one of the royal estates which rendered to the royal court not rent but the quantity of produce that would feed the court for one day - the "firma unius noctis", the farm of one night. After the building of the minster church it also became a great

Abbey tile

parish under royal patronage. By 1086 parts of the supposed original territory - perhaps Fareham and Alverstoke - had been carved off; the administrative unit called the Hundred of Titchfield then still included Wickham and Rowner. The "ancient parish" of later times was probably not clearly defined until the arrival of the Premonstratensians at the abbey. By the fourteenth century the boundary of the parish ran roughly from Curbridge along a small tributary of the Hamble river towards Shedfield, through Biddenfield to the river Meon near Knowle. Thence it followed the river to Hollam, but then turned sharply east between Fareham and Crofton to include the present site of H.M.S. Collingwood, and to Hoe Ford near Fleetlands on the Fareham to Gosport road. The boundary then went in a southerly direction to Peel Common and followed the river Alver to the sea at Browndown. It then returned to Curbridge all the way along the sea shore and the east bank of the Hamble river. This boundary remained substantially unchanged till the nineteenth century. As statutory duties were placed on this ancient ecclesiastical parish so it also became the civil parish of the nineteenth century, the largest in Hampshire.

Population growth in the nineteenth century saw the break up of the ancient parish. In 1837 the parish of Sarisbury was formed, including Swanwick, Burridge and Curbridge. In 1871 Crofton was formed and included Stubbington, Hill Head, Lee-on-the-Solent and Peel Common. The next year saw the formation of Hook-with-Warsash, and in 1893 Locks Heath was formed from parts of Warsash, Sarisbury and Titchfield. In 1930 Lee-on-the-Solent was separated from the rest of Crofton. As a result of these changes the very large ecclesiastical parish of Titchfield has now been reduced to a long strip about six miles long and one mile across lying largely to the west of the river Meon. The modern civil ward now also includes Catisfield, Ranvilles and the new Paul's Hill estate.

Within this parish lies a community which has always hovered on the borderline of the "large village" or "small town". What should we call it?

19

In the Middle Ages it had a town reeve: but at the dissolution of the monasteries, when Botley was referred to in Latin as a "burgus", Titchfield was referred to only as a "villa". It has never had a guild, a mayor, a corporation or a town charter, but it called itself a town in the vestry minutes and other papers of the eighteenth and early nineteenth centuries. Then, when the various modern local government divisions were created during the nineteenth century, Titchfield was growing much less quickly than neighbouring towns and so became part of Fareham Poor Law Union and ultimately of Fareham district. The word "town" ceased to be used about 1900, and all older people today talk about living in "the village"; that will be the term most frequently used in this volume.

This book does not attempt to tell the story of the whole of the ancient parish. To the west, the hamlets, and now rapidly growing modern townships, between the ancient common and the river Hamble - Hook, Warsash, Locks Heath, Park Gate, Sarisbury, Swanwick, Burridge and Curbridge - deserve a separate history of their own. So too, to the east, do the ancient villages of Crofton, Stubbington and Lee (once Lee Markes, now Lee-on-the-Solent). But for the present we confine ourselves as far as we can to Titchfield "town", to the modern ecclesiastical parish, and the area which lies along the river Meon from Great Funtley to the sea at Meon.

Domesday Book

The King holds TICEFELLE. It is a berewick, and belongs to MENES-TOCHES. King Edward held it. There are 2 hides; but they have not paid geld. (There) is land for 15 ploughs. In (the) demesne (there are) but 2 oxen (animalia), and (there are) 16 villeins and 13 bordars with 9 ploughs. There are 4 serfs, and a mill worth 20 shillings. The market and toll (are worth) 40 shillings.

In MENE the Bishop himself holds 1 hide; and it was assessed at so much. There is land for one plough, which is there with 2 villeins. There are 2 acres of wood with fences. It was, and is, worth 20 shillings. Tovi had half of this hide by (the act of) earl William (of Hereford); and the other part he had of the King for money ... And, on the same conditions as Tovi held ... this land, the Bishop enjoys it by the King's gift.

The Bishop himself holds BURNEWIC of the King, in fee. Angsgot held it of the Bishop. It does not belong to the Bishopric ... Edric held it of King Edward. It was then, and is now, assessed at 1 hide. There is land for 3 ploughs. In (the) demesne are 1½ ploughs; and (there are) 5 villeins and 11 bordars with 3 ploughs. There is 1 serf. It was always, and is, worth 4 pounds.

COUNT ALAN (of Brittany) holds CROFTONE. Ulward held it; and could betake himself ... where he would with this land. T.R.E. it was assessed at 7 hides; now at 3 hides less half a virgate. There is land for 5 ploughs. In (the demesne) is 1 plough; and (there are) 11 villeins and 2 bordars, with 4½ ploughs. There are a church and 4 serfs, and a mill worth 12 shillings and 6 pence; and 24 acres of meadow. There is wood(land) worth 5 swine. T.R.E. it was worth 8 pounds, and afterwards 100 shillings; (it is) now (worth) 4 pounds.

The same Count holds FUNTELEI, Ulward held it of Earl Godwin, and could not betake himself ... where he would. It was then, as now, assessed at 1 hide. There is land for 3 ploughs. There are 7 villeins and 2 serfs with 2½ ploughs; and a mill worth 10 shillings and 3 acres of meadow. T.R.E., and afterwards, it was worth 40 shillings; (it is) now (worth) 30 shillings. Eldred and the men of the Hundred testify that this manor does not belong to Croftune.

HUGH DE PORT holds SUGION (Segensworth); and Herlebald (holds it) of him. Ulvric held it of King Edward. It was then, as now, assessed at 1 hide. There is land for 3 ploughs. In (the demesne) is 1 plough; and (there are) 5 villeins and 2 bordars with 2 ploughs. There are 3 serfs, and a mill worth 20 shillings, and 5 acres of meadow. There is woodland worth 5 swine. T.R.E. it was, as now, worth 60 shillings. When received, it was worth 30 shillings.

ROBERT (son of Gerold) holds half a hide in FUNTELEI. Tovi held it of King Edward. It was then, as now, assessed at half a hide. There is land for 1 plough. There are 3 bordars and 6 acres of meadow. There is wood(land) worth 3 swine. It was, as now, worth 20 shillings.

RANNULF FLAMME holds FUNTELEI. Turi held it of Earl Godwine. It was then, as now, assessed at 1 hide; but there is 1 virgate of land more. There is land for 3 ploughs. In the demesne is 1 plough; and (there are) 4 villeins and 5 bordars with 2½ ploughs. There are 1 serf, and a mill worth 12 shillings and 6 pence, and 5 acres of meadow. There is wood(land) worth 10 swine. T.R.E. it was worth 4 pounds; it was afterwards, as now, worth 3 pounds.

The villages mentioned in this extract are Titchfield, Meon, Brownwich, Crofton, Funtley and Segensworth; there were three separate small estates at Funtley.

This translation of Domesday Book is taken from the *Victoria County History* of Hampshire. Some unusual words; a "berewick" was a subordinate estate; a "hide" was a unit of taxation, very roughly related to an area of land, sometimes 120 acres; a "virgate" was a holding of land in the common fields, of varying size, but often 32 acres; "geld" was a tax; "demesne" was the lord's home farm; "villeins" were tenants, holding perhaps 16 or 32 acres, who owed labour services to the lord; "bordars" were tenants of cottages or small pieces of land; "serfs" were slaves who worked as labourers on the demesne farms; "toll" was the lord's income from charges on market traders; "T.R.E." stood for "in the time of King Edward (the Confessor)", that is before the Norman Conquest and the short reign of Harold.

Harold riding to Bosham

22

The Normans

After the Jutes had been absorbed into the Saxon kingdom, the West Saxon, later the English, kings kept the village itself in their own hands. It is possible that they had a hunting lodge here as a base for hunting in the southern edge of the Forest of Bere. Before 1066 parts of the parish had been granted to other lords - Meon and Brownwich to the Bishop of Winchester, parts of Funtley to Harold's father, Earl Godwin; and the other estates to lesser noblemen. After the Norman conquest, William the Conqueror retained Titchfield and shared other parts of the parish amongst great Norman lords like Hugh de Port and Count Alan of Brittany.

Domesday Book, compiled in 1086, shows us a parish no longer largely covered by woodland and heath. Great stretches were occupied by arable land - land for fifteen ploughs (perhaps 2,000 acres) in Titchfield, for five ploughs at Crofton, for three ploughs at Brownwich and Segensworth, and so on. The grain grown on this land was ground by five water-mills at Titchfield, Funtley (two), Segensworth and Crofton, and some of it was sold in a market at Titchfield. The meadows along the Meon provided hay for cattle. In the remaining woodlands wandered herds of pigs, for which the rents were paid in kind. The lords had their home farms, sometimes called "demesne", on which much of the work was done by slaves or "serfs", though the demesne farm at Titchfield seems to have been neglected and derelict in 1086 (we still do not know where it was). The rest of the land was cultivated by the established village people, the "villein" families, who were expected to work for the lord as well as to pay him rents and other customary dues. We know that in later years much of their land was held as a number of strips (called in Titchfield "helums") in large common fields. As well as villeins, there were also people called in 1086 "bordars" who seem to have occupied cottages but only an acre or two of land: some of them were probably craftsmen and merchants. With their families, the villeins and bordars made up quite a large community - perhaps 150 people in Titchfield itself, and substantial numbers on the other estates. In the case of Brownwich there were in fact far more people than there are today! As well as the lesser Saxon landowners - men like Tovi and Turi - we also meet by name someone who may have been an ordinary villager - the Eldred who led the jury of men of the Hundred which compiled the Domesday information. The church at Crofton, which can still be visited, was mentioned in the survey, but the minster church at Titchfield was for some reason omitted.

An oddity of Domesday Book is that Titchfield is described as being an outlying estate ("berewick") of the smaller manor of Meonstoke. This may have been a distant memory of a time when the whole Meon valley was a Jutish kingdom; or it may have been merely a convenience for the collection of royal revenues. Odd or not, it was a detail which was to prove unexpectedly important two hundred years later when the abbot was quarrelling with his tenants.

Soon after 1086, the Conqueror's son, William Rufus, gave up the estate of Titchfield and granted it to the Norman nobleman Payn de Gisors, perhaps giving it up because the New Forest now provided all the hunting that the King needed in South Hampshire. It may have been one of the Gisors who made the "Norman" additions to the parish church, including the fine west doorway. The interesting fact about the family is that they were not just noblemen - they were merchants; and it may be that they acquired Titchfield as one of their bases for cross-channel trade. It was Payn's descendent John de Gisors who founded the new town of Portsmouth in 1180, so it is a fascinating possibility that the great modern port of Portsmouth was founded specifically to replace the muddy, twisting tidal channel of the Meon and its little harbour at Titchfield. At all events, John de Gisors backed the wrong side when Prince John intrigued against his absent brother Richard I, and forfeited both Portsmouth and Titchfield when the King returned. As one outcome, fifty years later, Peter des Roches, Bishop and powerful minister of John's son Henry III, was able to acquire Titchfield for the site of his new monastic house.

Norman doorway, St. Peter's Church

24

Titchfield Abbey

In 1232 Peter des Roches, Bishop of Winchester, invited a group of canons from the Premonstratensian Abbey of Halesowen in Worcestershire (which he had also founded) to establish a new community at Titchfield. We do not know why he chose this particular site, though it may have been intended at least in part as a respectable guest house accessible to Winchester, at the head of a tidal estuary and convenient for embarkation to France.

Abbey tile

Later bishops were to claim the right to lodge at the abbey whenever they returned from a journey overseas, and some important visitors used the abbot as a kind of travel agent, asking him to arrange their journeys from Southampton and elsewhere. The estuary also made it possible to import the stone from the Isle of Wight, Normandy and Dorset from which the abbey was built. Timber could be obtained from the woodland which covered the parish to the north of the abbey site.

Titchfield Abbey was of the Order of Prémontré, which had been founded in the early part of the twelfth century by St. Norbert. Norbert's followers were called canons and they based their rules on those of St. Augustine. To differentiate them from the Augustinian Order, which wore black, the founder of the Premonstratensian Order was given permission to clothe his canons in white. Hence their popular name - "White Canons". *Monks* are members of Orders which follow St. Benedict - Cluniacs and Benedictines (Black), Cistercians and Carthusians (White); *canons* are members of Orders which derived their rules from St. Augustine.

Those who visit the abbey expecting to see traces of its medieval splendour will be disappointed, for apart from an odd piece of wall here and there, patches of medieval tiles, a couple of wells and two abbots' graves, there is little to remind us that the ground was once covered with monastery buildings like those better preserved at Netley. However, as a result of the patient efforts of archaeologists at the beginning of this century, the ground plan has been fairly well established, though some of the original construction has been obscured by the later Tudor conversion to a nobleman's house.

Apart from those of the Carthusians, practically all abbeys and monasteries were based on a similar plan, which had as its main feature a *church* built in the shape of a Latin cross. The church was the centre of the whole abbey and every other part was complementary to it; it is significant that at the dissolution the churches of many monasteries (though not Titchfield) were left standing while the remaining buildings were torn down. Because the first and most important purpose of a monastery or abbey was to worship and glorify God, the church was the spiritual centre around which everything else revolved. It was here that the abbot and his canons spent much of their day, sitting in the canopied choir stalls and separated from the nave by a screen, which was often wonderfully carved and bore a crucifix. The ordinary people and lay-brothers worshipped in the nave, which effectively became a separate church. On Sundays and Saints' Days the canons, in solemn procession, would make their way through the cloisters, then into the nave, where they visited each altar sprinkling holy water while anthems were chanted.

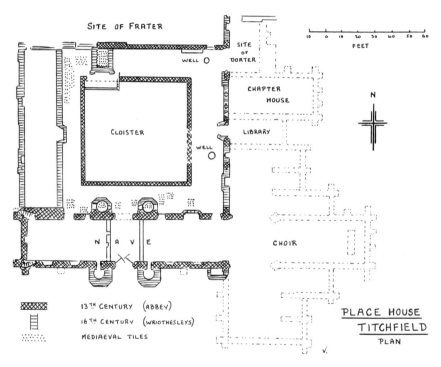

We know the locations of some, but not all, of the main rooms of the abbey (see the plan). The canons' bedroom the *dormitory* or *"dorter"* was situated as near the church as possible on the east side of the cloister, above the warming room and parlour. This arrangement enabled the canons to come down the "night stairs" into their places in the choir without exposing themselves to the elements. Such a provision seems essential when it is realised that every night they left the dorter at 2 a.m.

26

for the first service of Matins. The *warming-room* was the only place in the abbey where the canons could warm their hands and feet in winter, when the unheated church must have chilled their bones. The term *"parlour"* derives from the room in which the monks could meet relatives and callers from the outside world and talk more freely than in the cloisters.

Titchfield Abbey

Next to the church the chapter house was the most important part of the abbey, for it was here that following the late morning service the canons assembled. The abbot presided over the chapter, confessions were heard and punishment awarded - in some cases this might be a whipping with the birch. The business of granting charters, purchase of land, appointments of officials and general day-to-day organisation were all part of the duties of the chapter. While it was in session the doors were locked. Decisions were made by a show of hands in much the same way as at a modern committee. At Titchfield Abbey, the foundations of the chapter house are plain to see, and we can see that with its vaulted roof supported by elegant pillars and triple entrance arch with Purbeck marble shafts (still intact), it was originally a fine building.

Frater was a Norman-French word for the "refectory" or "dining room", an extension on the north side of the abbey. Today, unfortunately, only a small portion of the south wall is seen, for much of the remains in this area are in the grounds of the adjoining property and have not been uncovered. In the frater the canons met for their one or two meals each day, eaten in silence, while a junior member read aloud from the pulpit. There is an excellent example of a refectory with a pulpit and stairs at Beaulieu.

Before and after their meals the canons washed their hands in the *lavatory*, the name given to the washing place: a good illustration of how a word has

27

changed its meaning. The lavatory was a long room with a raised trough or sometimes even wash-basins made of stone or marble, supplied with running water and towels kept in a cupboard nearby. Washing was a strictly kept ritual, and abbeys often had piped water long before the houses of wealthy citizens.

All Premonstratensian establishments were headed by an *abbot*. The abbot was an important personage and wielded considerable authority in the neighbourhood. Sometimes he had the privilege of wearing a mitre and carrying a pastoral staff, just as a bishop does today. An unusual duty was to attend Parliament - a doubtful privilege - and instances are on record of abbots refusing to attend and even bribing the Clerk of Parliament not to summon them! The abbot was father of the house, not merely an earthly father but a spiritual father too. When he appeared all had to rise and bow as he passed by. When he returned from a long journey he would be met by all the canons and led in procession to the high altar where prayers of thanks would be said or chanted. He had great power and authority once he was elected, and held the position for life unless his health - or a misdemeanour - caused him to resign. In some abbeys he was assisted by a prior or assistant who was responsible for the day-to-day affairs of the abbey, seeing the lights were out and doors locked, and that the canons were in their stalls at the correct time.

A senior canon would be given the important position of *cellarer*. He had to supervise everything to do with food, drink and fuel, repairs to the abbey fabric and outlying farms, purchases of bacon, salt, dried fish and wine, iron, wood, ploughs and carts. All the details of the cost were set down in meticulous form. He also supervised all the employees of the abbey, including those on distant manors and granges, and his duties often caused him to be away from his seat in the choir.

The canon called the *kitchener* was in charge of all the meals served, and this, too, was a weighty responsibility. For the abbey not only had to feed its own people, but important travellers with large retinues would often demand hospitality. A quotation from "The Customs of Barnwell" - an early reference work on monastic matters - reads "the kitchener must see that all meals are served on time, the plates must be unbroken and not dirty on the underside so as to stain the tablecloth"!

The *hosteller's* duties were "to look after the guests and be hospitable, to see that the beds were clean and no spider webs in the guest house". He was to be there when travellers left to make sure they had left nothing behind and, more importantly, that they had not taken anything belonging to the abbey.

28

The brother in charge of the infirmary was the *almoner*. One of his duties, apart from looking after the sick, was to dispense alms, and the rule book already quoted said: "he was to give a special priority to pilgrims, chaplains, beggars and lepers and those down on their luck, remembering at all times that they were all God's creatures".

There was also a *librarian,* a particularly important post at Titchfield Abbey, which had an excellent library, housed in a small room next to the chapter house. The catalogue of this library still exists in the manuscript collection of the British Library in London. There were nearly a thousand works in the library, not printed of course, but painstakingly copied by hand and bound together into 224 volumes. Most of the works were of a religious nature, but a number also covered law and medicine, and there was an agricultural text book and one book of fables. The volumes were arranged in bookcases and numbered by the shelf and their order on the shelf - for instance shelf A, volume 4 was a Bible in verse. Volume P10 is now in the British Library and volume P13 is in the Hampshire Record Office.

In addition to these duties at the abbey, one canon normally served as the canon-vicar at Titchfield Church, another as the canon-chaplain of Crofton, and from time to time others lived as resident canon-bailiffs on outlying manors such as Inkpen in Berkshire.

This brief outline of its officials is sufficient to show what a busy institution an abbey was, especially when it is realised that although they were assisted by a large number of lay brothers and other servants there were never more than 14 canons resident at Titchfield at any one time.

We know a great deal about the abbey's estates but surprisingly little about its internal affairs and the lives of those who made up the community. Some light was however thrown on aspects of abbey life through the system of "visitations". We know that the abbey was ruled from 1231 to 1537 by a line of twenty abbots. It is likely that the plague of 1349 visited the abbey, for the abbot, Peter de Wynton, appointed only on 8 June 1348 died on 14 August 1349.

It was the head of the particular Order who sent visitors to report back on each of the daughter abbeys. In the case of Titchfield, the head of the Premonstratensian Order, living at Prémontré in France, appointed Bishop Redman, who was also Abbot of Shap in Cumberland, to visit Titchfield in 1478. He came to Titchfield on 2nd July and found a community of thirteen canons under Abbot William Austin living there. The bishop reported that the discipline was excellent and that he found nothing serious to correct or to report to his superior. He did, however, suggest that a better keeping of silence in the frater would help to attain greater perfection. The debt of the abbey was shown to be £40, but this was expected to be paid off soon. A good supply of provisions was seen in the storehouse. Four years later, Bishop Redman was again making his rounds, finding everything much the same - although the names on the register had changed somewhat. This time special commendation is passed on the abbot's administration: the old structure was in good repair and new buildings had been erected.

One amusing incident was brought to the bishop's notice. It was the case of one of the inmates, Ralph Axminster, who had left his dormitory at night to fish in the lake within the grounds. Why he did and whether he was punished for such a heinous offence we shall never know, but the site of the pond is there for all to see today.

Six more years pass before we read of the next visitation: by this time William Austin had been dead two years (1486), and Thomas Oke was now abbot. Again he reported that the abbey had a debt, this time £100. Bishop Redman made further visits in 1491, 1494, 1497 and 1502, but they add little fresh information to the abbey chronicles. The debt fluctuated from visit to visit, but it shows that the widely held belief that all the religious houses were extremely wealthy was untrue.

The next abbot was Thomas Blankepayne, who had entered the abbey as a boy. When he died in 1529, he had served the abbey for 46 years - remarkable when one considers the average span of life in those days.

John Max, Abbot of Welbeck in Nottinghamshire, was elected to follow Blankepayne, and in turn was succeeded by John Sympson in 1535. Sympson had the painful duty of presiding over the abbey during the preparations for its ignominious destruction in 1537. It is assumed that his appointment was connived at in order that he should prepare for the dissolution, although he did indeed resign in 1536.

An important feature of many abbeys were their fishponds, but it is very rare to find them today - or even traces of their sites. Here at Titchfield we are fortunate in being able to examine a series of ponds, recently restored by the owners of the adjacent Carron Row Farm.

Why were these ponds constructed? The answer lies in the vows which strictly governed the daily lives of all the monks and canons. Among the vows which governed their eating was one which said that no fresh meat was to be consumed. There were some exceptions, such as when canons were in hospital; then pittances (small amounts of fresh meat) could be prescribed for certain ailments - or awarded by the abbot as a special treat. As one alternative they turned to fish; and to ensure a constant supply for the abbey kitchens many ponds were essential.

To find suitable places where the ponds could be located was not always easy, but at Titchfield there was a convenient valley running to the back of the abbey, parallel with Segensworth Road. In this area the canons set up a fish farm. It perhaps originally consisted of five ponds, each one connected to the one below by a spillway, so that each when full allowed water to be fed into the one below. The dams were made by felling large oaks and laying them across the floor of the valley to form a base for the retaining dam. Huge quantities of earth, excavated from inside the pond, were necessary to raise the banks to the required height and to make them strong enough to withstand the pressure as the water level built up.

Numerous species of freshwater fish were used to stock the ponds: roach, carp, eels and perch were recorded as suitable for the table. The amount of information about this aspect of monastic activities is very sparse and little research on the management of fishponds appears to have been carried out.

Another important purpose of the abbey ponds was the provision of a constant supply of water. Nowadays we take for granted an unlimited supply of clean water in every house, but the canons had to devise their own means of providing the large quantities necessary for the needs of their establishment. From the corner of the lowest pond, (which has not yet been restored, as it is under different ownership), a brick conduit channels the water under the abbey wall where it would have been piped to various locations, such as the kitchens, brewhouse, lavatory (wash house) and stables. The toilets (rere-dorter) were also flushed. The channel must have drained into the river near the Fisherman's Rest. Netley Abbey still has a good example of the arrangement, complete with running water.

The abbey, having been the lord and landowner of Titchfield for just over 300 years, was finally formally surrendered to the Crown on 28 December 1537. It was then said to have in its possession the manors of Titchfield, Abshot, Posbrook, "Newcourt Parva", Fontley, Swanwick, Crofton, Mirabell, Newland, Wallsworth, Portsea, Copnor, Cadland, Corhampton, Wicor in Portchester and Inkpen in Berkshire; and other land in Wickham, "Warsashfield", Brook, Portchester and elsewhere; with the churches of Titchfield, Lomer and Corhampton. The site of the abbey and the estates were granted to Thomas Wriothesley.

31

Titchfield about 1300

The parish continued to grow in prosperity after the foundation of the abbey. In the manor of Titchfield the Domesday Book population of perhaps 150 people had at least quadrupled by 1300 and still went on growing. In place of the single run-down demesne farm of 1086, the abbey had established three separate farms of its own. One of these was Great Posbrook; the locations of the other two are less certain, but the "Rectory Barton" was probably the later Fernhill Farm, and "Lee" may have been the modern Carron Row. Between them, these three home farms had, at the height of their prosperity, about 1,000 acres of land under the plough, producing wheat, barley and oats, and some 1,500 sheep, kept for the value of their wool rather than their meat. The tenant farmers of the manor themselves cultivated another 1,500 acres and also had about the same number of sheep, which grazed on the common in the summer and on the corn stubble after the harvest.

As well as being the centre of a busy agricultural district, Titchfield was a substantial market town by medieval standards. The court rolls of the abbey show us that it was crowded with all kinds of people. In the village lived the administrative staff of the estates, the bailiff, a reeve, a town reeve, clerks, porters and abbey servants. In small cottages near the demesne farmsteads and along the road to the abbey lived the ploughmen, carters, dairymen, shepherds and huntsmen of the demesne; and the hired experts, the ditchers, threshers, sowers and mowers. There were the most usual of the craftsmen, the smiths and the iron workers, and of course the miller. In and around the market square, cooks, butchers, bakers, brewers and salters, did an active business supplying the abbey and its visitors as well as the countryside. In the yards and alleys between the square and the church were the workshops of carpenters and coopers, roofers and thatchers, bowl makers and rope makers, tailors and barbers. Then there were two particular groups which may reasonably be regarded as forming local industries, those using leather - skinners, tanners, leather dressers, harness makers, saddlers and shoemakers, who may have had their workshops along the river between the church and the mill where the nineteenth century tannery stood; and those preparing wool - fullers, treaders, combers, spinners and dyers. The settlement of the merchants, sailors and substantial freeman we also find in the village was the natural consequence of all this commercial activity.

There had been a market at Titchfield since at least 1086, though the five-day fair was not granted until 1447. Titchfield village was referred to as a market town, *villa mercatoria* in a court of 1335, and there was a town reeve, *praepositus burgi,* as well as a manorial reeve by at least 1329. As we would expect from the products of local farming, butchers and bakers were the most common of the tradesmen, eight butchers and a baker for instance being fined for overcharging in the Titchfield court of 1398. The trade in live animals, hides and leather, wool and wool fells was obviously connected with this traffic in meat, just as the trade in bread, flour and grain was connected with the business of the bakers. Fish, from the fishponds, from around the coasts and from the rivers were sold in the market. Beer was brewed by many tenants, and beer and wine were sold in the taverns which are mentioned; we also hear of tolls being paid on sales of cider. Hemp and flax were mentioned in the tithe arrangements of 1264-75, and the manufacture of hemp is associated with the 'ropers' who appear among the villagers. The shops and workshops of these people were of course only cottages; the largest commercial buildings were the mills, which also dealt in grain and flour, and the fulling mill at Fontley Furstbury.

Two major products of the area were timber and salt, and again the tenants and not just the abbot took part in the production and sale of both. The court rolls record continual fines for cutting and selling timber without licence. For instance in the Swanwick court in 1308 William Reve of Curbridge took over his father's land and shortly after was fined for felling oaks without licence. In 1310 he was forbidden to make a passage across his land for timber or other merchandise, "lest the king's customs should be impaired or a highway to the sea claimed". In 1313, however, he was given permission to have a "port" on his land at Curbridge for two years. William was obviously an energetic timber merchant as well as a farmer. The other local product, salt, was manufactured all along the coast. Salt pans (*salinae*) were held by tenants at Cosham, Portchester, Titchfield, Swanwick and Cadland. Salt was sent from Titchfield to the abbey's manor at Inkpen on a number of occasions, and it is interesting to note that the Bishop of Winchester's manor of Bursledon, across the Hamble from Swanwick, similarly sent salt to three of the Bishop's other manors in the county.

Medieval Titchfield was not only a very busy place, it was also in constant contact with the outside world. The abbey kept in touch with most of its local estates by sea as well as by road. Given a favourable wind, Southampton was only about half an hour's journey by boat from Cadland near Hythe and some ten miles by road or an hour by sea from Titchfield and Swanwick. The 'fleet' of Hook and the Hamble estuary on which Swanwick and Warsash in Titchfield lay were important roadsteads for shipping. The tenants of Swanwick and Warsash in fact carried the abbot to Hook, Cadland and Southampton as one of their services. Then as now the sea was the obvious outlet for the landless men of the local villages. At

Cadland, for instance, in 1320 Robert Pynnock was reported to have been detained in "transmarine parts" by contrary winds since before the last court. In 1349 it was reported that John Broun of Cadland had been captured at sea in time of war by the enemies of the king and taken outside the realm of England and had not returned. At Crofton in 1351 the death was reported of Simon Havek who had held a messuage and virgate of land and whose heriot (death payment) was a mare; he had been killed at sea by enemies from Normandy. His father Robert now took the tenement until Michaelmas, having the right to the corn of every kind which was sown there, and Roger Foxore paid a mark - 13s. 4d or 67p - to have it thereafter. In 1359 it was said that William Hoggyn who had been pledged by his brother, his brother-in-law, a kinsman and two others to stay in his house and pay the dues called chevage, carrying on his seaman's business, *officium naute*, had after all left the demesne. At Swanwick in 1355 William Sexi had to undertake that he would not take himself off to overseas parts without licence, and that when he returned from the voyage for which he was then licensed, if he was still alive, he would engage in agriculture with his neighbours. In the abbey's rental Nicholas son of John Saltere of Crofton appears as paying 6d (2½p) annual capitage to be allowed to stay at Dartmouth or Plymouth but only at the will of the lord.

The distances which the tenants travelled by land appear most clearly in the Portchester custumal. The tenants there had to go for the lord's food to Southampton, Winchester or Chichester; if they were "abroad" through the night their expenses were paid by the abbot, and they were quit of two days' work for the service. If the lord bought seed at Titchfield, Fareham, Southwick or elsewhere the tenants had to carry it to Portchester and were excused a day's work. They had to take the corn to be ground at the mill of Wickham or of Fontley, or if the lord wished to sell, to the markets of Fareham, Titchfield or Southwick. The Titchfield tenants had to carry food to Winchester.

The market attracted men to Titchfield from all the neighbouring villages; selling meat there in 1398 were John Boucher of Wickham, Thomas Boucher of Chilling, Thomas Neel of Rowner and William Martin of Portchester. There were at least two smiths from other villages working there: Henry Faber of Fareham had a holding in 1275, and John de Northbrook of Wallworth, smith, took up a piece of demesne for customs like those of the other cottars in 1335.

There were in fact many immigrants living in medieval Titchfield. The names of the people who appeared in the abbey's records show us that the seaborne traffic along the Hampshire coast came from far afield, from Sussex and Kent and the Thames estuary on one side, and from Devon and

Cornwall and the Severn on the other, and through Southampton came Scots, Irish, Spaniards, Frenchmen, Rhinelanders and Flemings. Men from far beyond these normal limits, from Kenilworth and Whitby, for instance, had probably first come with the armies embarking at Southampton and Portsmouth for the French wars, and on their return had preferred to settle in the busy little ports where they disembarked rather than to make the long journey back to the north.

Many immigrants from the interior of Hampshire can be identified among the local residents at this time. Why did small farmers, peasants and labourers make the two or three day journey from downland villages like Kingsclere and Somborne to look for land and work in the coastal villages? In some cases we can see what happened. In the year of the Black Death Thomas Scad of Tuderle (Tytherley in Hampshire) a carter, married Johanna, daughter of Robert Peeke of Crofton, without licence; no more is heard of either of them and he presumably took her back to Tytherley with his load. If she had stayed a little longer and paid the marriage fine he could have settled down there, for two of her relations had died in the plague and one of the tenements had fallen in hand. At Titchfield in 1335 Johanna Stopeham (Stopham is thirty miles away in Sussex) died, a cottar whose heriot was a ewe worth 9d; her cottage fell in hand and was taken up by John le Kembere (the comber) of Husseborn (Hurstbourne is nearly thirty miles to the north). John may have been an itinerant worker in wool who took the chance afforded by the death of Johanna, probably herself a spinster, to get a cottage and workshop.

It was perhaps, as it may have been in the fifteenth century and was in the eighteenth and nineteenth centuries, the lure of the towns which induced people to move. Southampton, Portsmouth, Portchester, Titchfield and Wickham were among the most heavily assessed of the Hampshire towns in 1333, and the Hampshire towns compared favourably in wealth with those of other counties. There was a thriving coastal and overseas trade, important fairs and markets were held in towns, and as has been seen, there were small industries based on local raw materials. It is easy to see why small traders, craftsmen and pedlars would tend to drift south or use a workshop in a coastal town as a base when collecting and distributing in the downland villages. A further point is that the gravels and clays of the coastal region, settled and cleared later than many of the downland villages, were richer than the chalk lands to the north. On the Titchfield estates there was still land being brought into cultivation, while in the upland villages the remaining waste land may have been too poor even for temporary cultivation. There is some evidence in fact that the population of these manors was increasing in the first half of the fourteenth century when that of other parts of the country may have been declining. If there was work to be found for skilled and seasonal labour there, the poor cottager with all his wealth on his back may have thought of the coastal towns as Irishmen thought of nineteenth century England. Finally, as holdings by free and "soke" tenure were as common on these estates as holdings in strict villeinage, and labour services were often light and frequently commuted, there was an added inducement for the wealthy upcountry peasant to saddle his horse and make the overnight journey to Titchfield, to enquire of the abbey and in the market and taverns about vacant holdings, or the possibility of a sale. After the Black Death migration in search of better and cheaper land became even more common. But it was in the century or so between the foundation of the abbey and the coming of the plague that Titchfield reached the highest point of population and prosperity in its history, relatively that is to the rest of the country and to towns like Winchester and Southampton. In the six hundred years since then, its population first fluctuated and then grew, but much more slowly than that of the great urban centres. Titchfield the prosperous town of 1300 was never to grow into Titchfield the city.

Cloister Ruins, Titchfield Abbey

The Abbey versus the Villagers

About a dozen years after the abbey's foundation, the abbot seems to have decided that it was time to ask his tenants for more rents and services: possibly because the cost of erecting the fine abbey church and the extensive abbey buildings had proved to be greater than expected. Not unnaturally, his tenants from the first showed little sympathy with this new

Abbey tile

landlord's financial problems, and resisted his demands. The first hint of trouble we have is from 1246, when the Titchfield tenants paid a large sum of money not to have to carry the lord's hay and corn for him; and in 1256 the tenants at Posbrook and Meon were fined in the manorial court for refusing to perform the same service. At the same time at Swanwick, on the other side of the common, we are told that there was a *querela* (quarrel) between the abbot and the tenants there which had to be taken to one of the courts in London.

In 1272 the friction in Titchfield broke out into a major dispute which then led to a long-lasting law-suit. The Titchfield tenants refused to pay various sums of money or to do certain extra services which the abbot was insisting were due to him. They claimed that they were not mere "villeins" at all, but a class of tenants called "sokemen" whose rents and services were by custom fixed and permanent. The abbot of course contested this. But it was generally admitted that the tenants of estates which had once belonged to the king *were* sokemen, and of course Titchfield *had* belonged to the king at the time of Domesday Book. We know that the lawyers for both sides went to London and looked at Domesday Book itself. The villagers were of course delighted and the royal court actually gave a verdict for them, but the abbot's lawyers had now spotted a loophole. They saw in Domesday Book that Titchfield was, for some obscure reason, described as part of Meonstoke. So they went up to Meonstoke and found what the rents and services there were. Of course, the Meonstoke services turned out to be more onerous than anyone had ever done in Titchfield - but once the villagers had made use of Domesday Book they could hardly go back on it. In fact, they continued to argue, and in the end, in 1276, a compromise was worked out. The long-established villagers agreed to pay quite high rents, but the abbot on his part accepted that these rents should be fixed and not increased again. At the time of course this was to the abbot's advantage; but over many years it turned out to be in the tenants' interest. Strangely though, those tenants who had only recently arrived in the village (between 1232 and 1272) were not included in the 1276 agreement.

They were instead allowed to keep the lower rents and services which had been normal when they came into the village: these were called the "old customs". Those of the established families were called the "new customs". This distinction between the old and the new customs was remembered for over six hundred years, in fact, until the 1920's. People in Titchfield today who look carefully at the deeds of their properties will find that until quite recently they might have owed to the lord of the manor the "old" customs of 1232 or even the more up-to-date "new" customs - of 1276!

Arguments between the abbot and his Titchfield tenants were not ended by the compromise of 1276. In 1319, for instance, Robert le Small and his three sons John, William and Roger were reported to have insulted one of the canons: they were brought to the manorial court, but only made matters worse there by behaving badly in front of the cellarer and the steward. Their fellow-villagers would seem to have sympathised with the Smalls, because a dozen of them were accused of holding a "conventicle" to discuss the matter and later of being involved in a conspiracy against the king's peace. And when in 1320 the abbot tried to get a jury of the free tenants (not villeins or sokemen) to bring a verdict against the conspirators, the freemen refused to do so. We do not know in fact how this particular case ended.

Thirty years later in 1352, the abbot made the mistake of employing a corrupt bailiff, a man called John Pouke, to collect his rents. We know that he was indeed corrupt because the tenants both at Titchfield and at Portchester gleefully reported his various misdemeanours in their courts. But at Titchfield matters went somewhat further - three villagers stopped Pouke in the street, insulted him and whipped him. Towards the end of the century, the strong feelings of local people were expressed even in the parish church. When one of the bishop's officers, after mass on 23 December 1377, stood up to announce the closure of a small chapel at the hamlet of Hook, the congregation shouted him down. The Hook chapel was not in fact shut. In another incident in 1400 the local people there turned out with bows and arrows to prevent the abbot's officers once again from closing it. This Hook chapel, now long disappeared, probably just fell into disrepair as the population of that hamlet dwindled in the fifteenth century. But at Hook, as at Swanwick and at Titchfield, we have a great deal of evidence of the robust and forthright character of our medieval ancestors.

The Black Death in Titchfield

In the 1340's the disease called plague, which had not been known in Europe for 500 years, spread like a forest fire across Asia and Europe, and arrived in England in the late summer of 1348. This terrible epidemic came to be known as the Black Death. It remained as an endemic disease in England until the late seventeenth century, when the plague of London in 1665 is usually taken as marking the end of that particular long-lasting outbreak. Smaller isolated outbreaks have occurred since.

Plague has a number of forms: one, pneumonic plague, can be spread by coughing or sneezing; but the commonest form, bubonic plague, signalled by dark lumps on the body, seems to be most often spread by fleas living on rats. The spread of the plague is thought to have been connected with the development of medieval trade and agriculture, and the movement of carts and ships loaded with grain - and with rats.

Titchfield may have been one of the first places in England to suffer from the plague. The traditional date for its arrival in England is June 1348 in Weymouth: it was probably raging in Titchfield by September, for a large number of deaths were reported in the October and November manorial courts. We can guess that the infection had come to Titchfield direct by ship from France rather than overland from Dorset or one of the nearby towns. The plague raged in Titchfield throughout the winter, a very large number of deaths being reported in the March court of 1349, and further deaths in May. Altogether, the deaths of 123 Titchfield tenants were reported in those two years, and since there were probably no more than 150 tenants before the plague, the mortality among tenants may have been as high as 80%. What the mortality was amongst children, women and people too poor to be tenants we do not know. In the remote hamlet of Quob north of Funtley everyone died. In a Titchfield court of 1350 it was reported that "to this court came Thomas Schad for the tithingman of Quob and witnessed that all and each of the tithing died in the present pestilence and that all the land and tenements within the bounds have come into the hand of Lord John des Roches (the local landowner) who sent the said Thomas to this day for the tithingman; he is in mercy but is pardoned and it is presented that all is well ...". It was three years before anyone appeared at the Titchfield court to speak for Quob.

Outbreaks of the plague did not cease in 1349. There was a further epidemic in 1360-61, another in 1374, and more in later years. Through their appearances in the courts, we can see how these outbreaks affected particular Titchfield families. The Sweins, for instance, were probably the most important family group in Titchfield before 1349, six or more of the family normally holding land, and the family must have consisted of thirty or more individuals in 1348. Six Swein tenants died in the first plague and two in the plague of 1360-61; these two were succeeded by their widows, neither of whom had children surviving at their deaths. The last known Swein of the fourteenth century, Alice widow of Roger, died at the very end of Edward III's reign, and her land was taken by another villager (though, in fact, the Sweins reappeared in Titchfield in later centuries, perhaps by the return of a distant relative from a nearby village).

The Frends, a small family group with three branches before the Black Death, lost two tenants in the first plague and two in the second and were wiped out before 1379, disappearing entirely from Titchfield history. On the other hand the Kechs, who were one of the most important local family groups, with four or five tenants before the Black Death, had the extreme good fortune of coming through all the outbreaks up to 1377 without losing a tenant; in the rental of that year their principal representatives John and Henry Kech both appear with holdings they had collected from other families, John with holdings of 32, 10 and 8 acres, and Henry with 32 and 14 acres. The Hirchons, a smaller family group which had only branched out into several separate families in the 1320s were fortunate in quite a different way. They lost five members in the first plague, but came unscathed through the later outbreaks and showed great powers of recovery, having apparently inexhaustible resources of sons who took up less fortunate people's vacant holdings wherever possible. In 1377 William, Thomas and Richard Hirchon all held 32 acre virgates, and two Roger Hirchons had smaller holdings.

People who survived the plagues then were often better off. But in general the population was lower, the market for goods of all kinds was smaller, and there was a long period of economic depression, in Titchfield as elsewhere in the country. The population of the parish for two hundred years remained lower than it had been in 1349. We can trace the economic effects of the plague epidemics in the records of the abbey's demesne farms as well as in the lives of its tenants. In 1348, for instance, the abbey had on all its estates 3,876 sheep; in 1390 it had only 2,859 and in 1420 only 1,396. Of oxen, cows, horses and pigs it had in 1348 a total of 810, in 1390 706, and in 1420 only 535. One important source of income affected by this decline was the sale of wool. We know that early in the fourteenth century the abbey had been selling to Italian merchants every year an average of 15 sacks of wool worth in all £90: that income must have fallen to £30 or £40 a century later. The abbey ceased to be the energetic and ambitious landlord it had been for the first hundred years of its existence. It was glad to collect what rents it could; some of its buildings fell into disrepair, and it was sometimes in debt. It interfered less and less often with the activities of

40

tenants, who seem to have been allowed, for instance, to enclose their common fields and to fell their trees much more freely than in the years before the Black Death. Most strikingly, after a time the canons ceased to make those careful notes of their business and possessions which survive today to tell us so much about the village in the fourteenth century. As a result, we at present know relatively little about Titchfield in the fifteenth century, and there is still much research to be done.

Fourteenth century drawing

The Tithe Barn

The great barn which stands to the south-west of Place House and the abbey ruins is popularly known as the tithe barn; but we in fact have no evidence that the storage of the tithes of corn was its main purpose - it may simply have been a normal working barn attached to the abbey's home farm, in recent times called Fernhill Farm. After the parish church and the gatehouse of Place House, this is the finest piece of architecture in the parish, the sweeping lines of its exterior contrasted with depth and height of the interior. We do not at present know the precise date of its construction; it was certainly there in 1610. The style of construction and basic materials employed remained in use for several centuries, but some experts have suggested the late fifteenth century as the most likely date. This points historically to William Austin as the abbot perhaps responsible: in the late fifteenth century Austin (1470-85) worked hard to restore the declining grandeur of the abbey, building amongst other things the "Great Place", the building now in ruins in the meadow immediately west of Place House. The south and west walls of the barn seem to have been rebuilt later, perhaps on two occasions, using both brick and stone taken from the derelict abbey.

The barn is 46 feet wide and 157 feet long, divided into eight bays each of approximately 20 feet. The floor area is thus nearly 7,000 square feet, and the roof is covered by 70,000 tiles. The two doors on the east side are larger than those on the west, the wagons coming in loaded on that side and passing out empty on the other. The bays between the pairs of doors were used for threshing in the winter months, the doors being opened to allow the dust and chaff to be blown through and away from the flailers. The village corn mill is of course only a short distance below the barn in the valley below. In the nineteenth century, the north end of the barn was converted as a stable and for general storage, and a byre was built against the east side. The main part of the barn was in use for its original purpose until the mid-1950's, one of the present writers having stacked corn and straw there at that time. For several years in the 1960's the barn was disused, and in danger of decay, but the present owners have co-operated with public bodies in a fine restoration programme (1980). The barn now forms part of the premises of the Titchfield Abbey Fruit Farm and can be visited by patrons of the farm.

Titchfield about 1550

Soon after the conversion of Titchfield Abbey into Place House was complete, Thomas Wriothesley in 1546 ordered a detailed survey to be made of his newly-acquired properties. We can compare this with the survey which the abbot had made in 1377 after the first three major plague epidemics, so that, as well as giving us interesting details of the parish in 1546, we can get some impression of the effect of some two hundred years of endemic plague.

Titchfield itself, the local market town and port, had managed to maintain itself during that time: 86 tenants are listed in 1546 as compared with 88 in 1377. The medium-sized villages in the parish, however, such as Crofton and Swanwick, had lost about a quarter of thier tenants; the smaller villages of 1377 - like Funtley and Segensworth - were no longer villages at all but merely groups of farmhouses; and several of the smallest communities - for instance, three hamlets called Field, Pleistow and Shethedge, all on the western edges of the common - had disappeared for ever.

Within Titchfield, the 1546 Survey gives us our first picture of the street system. Many of the tenements are described as lying along the High Street (17 tenements), West Street (17 tenements), South Street (14 tenements) and East alias Church Street (7 tenements). The modern East Street and Mill Street (formerly called North Street) are not mentioned at that date. We also hear of Frog Lane (gentrified to Castle Street only in recent years), the lane leading to the Garston, and the lane from Hunt Pond to the town (Common Lane). The survey for the first time enables us to locate two inns. The George is described as standing at the north corner of the Warebridge (also known as Varman's Bridge), and obviously bore the same relationship to the little tidal port that the Horse and Jockey still has to the upper Hamble at Curbridge. The inn in West Street is called the Inn House, and may have been on the site of the present Old Inn House, later the first West End Inn. One house can also be identified for the first time: the tenement called Maybrayes, presumably the modern Mayburys. Two interesting tenement names which have disappeared were Elyas Grove, and Northes, a tenement belonging to the lord of the manor of Brownwich. Another now forgotten name was Stephanbridge: this was the bridge over the ditch or rivulet which crosses the Meon Road just south of Bellfield, and it gave its name to a common field there.

The survey shows us the old common fields of the village at a further stage in their slow decay: the arable fields were never formally enclosed as they were in some other villages. That a field was still called a common field did not imply that the land was cultivated in common: plots were described as "enclosed but in the common field". The Garston, the block of land south of West Street and west of South Street, was still described as a common field; as was Stephanbridge; so too were fields first heard of in medieval records like the Northfield, the Southfield, Hardbeating and Sheephill. But much of the land was now in closes like the seven closes of Crofton which Thomas White held. The decay of the old system had been recently accelerated by the extension of the great park of Place House; the tenants who had been dispossessed of land for this extension had been given in exchange pieces of the old common lying around Hunt Pond and along the lane to Hunt Pond which had been enclosed for that purpose. At Posbrook and Meon on the other hand the old system seems still to have been operating (Posbrook is described as "Posbrook alias Meon Manor"). The land holdings there were described as virgates, half or quarter virgates; and surprisingly a "virgate" was defined as 10 acres (in Titchfield it had been 32 acres in earlier times). We have a few glimpses in this survey of the trade of the village: several tenants were paying rent for market stalls as well as for their houses: and the William Osmond who had a cottage at a forgotten location called Dunbridge was called a carpenter to distinguish him from the more important William Osmond, who was the bailiff.

Medieval Buildings

44

The Earls of Southampton

In December 1537 Titchfield Abbey and the estates came into the hands of Thomas Wriothesley, at the age of 32 one of Henry VIII's most faithful officials. "Wriothesley" was a gentrified form of the family name of "Writh", and was pronounced "Risley". The Wriothesleys had for many years been royal servants: Thomas' grandfather, Sir John, had officiated at Henry VII's coronation; his uncle, another Sir Thomas, had been Garter-King-at-Arms; and his

Wriothesley arms

father, William, had been York Herald. Thomas himself had been at the royal court since the age of eighteen, acting as secretary both to Thomas Cromwell and to the King himself during the difficult years of his divorce from Catherine of Aragon. He had a house at Micheldever, and had taken an interest in several of the local monasteries, so that when the monasteries were dissolved it was not surprising that he should have obtained first some of the lands of Quarr Abbey on the Isle of Wight, then Titchfield, then Beaulieu, and later Hyde Abbey in Winchester. As on his other estates, Thomas acted with great speed at Titchfield in ordering the conversion of the abbey into a residence. By the time John Leland, the traveller, passed through Titchfield in 1542 he was able to write "Mr. Wriothesley hath builded a right stately house embattled and having a goodely gate and a conducte (conduit) casteled in the middle of the courte of it, yn the very same place where the late Monasterie of the Premonstratenses stoode". Wriothesley was not the only one in a hurry to see the abbey gone. Within a few days of the surrender, a man named Sherlond and half-a-dozen neighbours turned up, offering to buy statues, altars and stone. The tenants came in such large numbers to renew their leases with the new landlord that the parish church had to be used as the manor court. They were said to be glad that the abbey had been dissolved, and the report that they said that it should have been done seven years before has the authentic sound of Titchfield voices in it. Wriothesley was assured by his agent that "you have now many good and hearty tenants, divers of them good archers". The only hesitation was shown in the demolition of the steeple of the abbey church: it was in a dangerous state, it was mid-winter, the carpenter delayed and, superstitiously, the agent said "we would be loth to adventure with him before the change in the moon".

Thomas Wriothesley probably spent relatively little time at Titchfield. After the dissolution he remained an active royal officer. He was knighted in 1540, became Baron Titchfield in 1544, and was left £500 in Henry VIII's will. In the early months of Edward VI's reign, Wriothesley retained much power, becoming Earl of Southampton in 1547, but was involved in the political rivalries of that reign, and was in some disgrace when he died in his house in Holborn, London, in 1550. One of the issues was that in the developing religious division of those years some of the Wriothesleys remained for many years either Catholics or Catholic sympathisers.

Thomas' son Henry was aged only five when he succeeded to the title; seven when he was host to Edward VI at Titchfield in 1552; and only 20 when he married. Although Henry entertained the young Queen Elizabeth at Titchfield in 1569, he was later involved in a number of Catholic plots against the queen, and as a result spent several years in the Tower. Henry was perhaps fortunate in 1581 to die in his bed at Titchfield, though at the early age of 37. In his will he left moneys for the erection of the fine monument in the parish church.

His son, another Henry, was not quite eight when he in his turn succeeded, becoming the third Earl. As a boy he was a royal ward, in the guardianship of Elizabeth's powerful minister Lord Burghley. Henry grew up to be a handsome and cultured courtier, friend of the young Earl of Essex and patron of several writers, including William Shakespeare. Wriothesley may in those years have spent little time at Titchfield: as well as the London palace, Southampton House, in Holborn, he had several other houses. Towards the end of Elizabeth's reign, Henry, now in his twenties, engaged in several rash escapades which culminated in a very dangerous involvement in Essex's unsuccessful rebellion of 1601. Henry, like his father before him, was lucky to escape with his life and to suffer nothing worse than imprisonment in the Tower until the Queen's death two years later.

The third Earl was released from the Tower by James I, but he was not by nature the kind of patient, industrious official his grandfather had been, and so in the new reign became not a courtier but a politician and active member of the House of Lords. Southampton was a vigorous, restless man, at times hot-tempered, at others charming and companionable. Among his many interests was the exploration and settlement of North America, and nearer home as Captain of the Isle of Wight he spent much time at Carisbrooke Castle improving the defences of the Island. But he also found time to take a close interest in his house and estate at Titchfield. It was Henry who built the canal, the Stony Bridge and the ironworks; had the estate surveyed and the great map made; who almost certainly built the market hall; who is said to have revived the woollen industry and probably set up the "clothing-house", a workshop or small factory which was mentioned in 1634. And his efforts appear to have been successful: the parish registers show that the population of the parish rose steadily from the late sixteenth century to the 1640's. The third Earl himself died, aged 51, in 1624 on a military campaign in Holland: with him died his elder son.

The Wriothesley Monument

47

The fourth Earl, Henry's second son Thomas, succeeded to the estates at the age of 17, and shortly after entertained Charles I and his newly married Queen, Henrietta Maria, at Titchfield. He had at first been critical of the royal government, but by the beginning of the Civil War had joined the king. He remained a moderate and several times took part in negotiations between the combatants. In spite of the earlier disagreements the royal couple retained fond memories of Titchfield and the king fled here during his attempt to escape from parliamentary control. It was in fact while he was hiding at Place House in 1647 that he was found by Colonel Hammond and taken into custody. The fourth Earl is said to have sat with the king's body through the night after the execution. He was allowed to live quietly at Titchfield during the Commonwealth and Protectorate. At the Restoration Charles II appointed him Lord Treasurer, but he lost sympathy with Charles's policies. Thomas died in London in 1667. Both of his sons had died in childhood. Of his surviving daughters, one married the Earl of Gainsborough and took the house at Titchfield into that branch of the family: Charles II visited them there in 1675. Another daughter married the Duke of Montagu, and their descendant still lives in another of the family houses at Beaulieu. Titchfield was to pass to the Dukes of Beaufort, one of whom sold the estate to the Delmé family in 1741.

But in the late 17th and early 18th centuries the owners visited the house less and less frequently, and then only on their way to the coast. Parts of the house seem to have been occupied from time to time by dowagers and other female relatives, but some parts were allowed to fall into disrepair. When Missing wrote his poem in 1740 he could already describe the house as "sunk in dust". The fortunes of the great house were paralleled in those years by the fortunes of the parish. For still obscure reasons the Civil War and its aftermath appear to have done long term damage to the economy of the village. Although the diarist Pepys, when he rode down Hollam Hill in April 1662 said that "in one view we could see £6000 per annum" we can assume he was exaggerating, for he was a political opponent and thus a jealous critic of the fourth Earl. The population of the parish in fact fell steadily through the late 17th century, only recovering in the middle of the eighteenth. The village legend that the figure on the bonfire is that of the third Earl, burnt because he closed off the estuary, is however almost certainly a fabrication; more likely to be genuine are those memories which recall a golden age in which the energetic Earl had revived the woollen industry and brought a generation of prosperity to the village.

Shakespeare and Titchfield

That William Shakespeare knew the third Earl of Southampton is undoubted: both his poems *Venus and Adonis* and *The Rape of Lucrece* were dedicated to the young Henry Wriothesley. But that he knew Titchfield well is a much more doubtful matter, although there are all kinds of stories about the Shakespeare connection: that *Romeo and Juliet* was based on a family feud in Titchfield; that *Romeo and Juliet* was first performed in the ancient barn; that Shakespeare himself acted in the barn; and so on. There is little doubt that these stories were often extemporised over a pint of Abbey Ale for the gratification of visiting antiquarians. It is not a coincidence that they only make an appearance in the late nineteenth century, after members of the Hampshire Field Club and others began to visit the village.

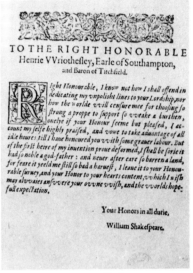

Dedication by Shakespeare
to Henry Wriothesley

It is possible to trace to their source two particular stories: the first was the 'fact' that the unusual surname 'Gobbo' (which Shakespeare used in *The Merchant of Venice*) appears frequently in the parish registers. The story of this 'fact' is an instructive study in the development of historical myth. It was not mentioned by the poet Missing, who was anxious to find any reason for praising his native village; it is not even mentioned in the first parish guidebook, *Some Notes on Titchfield Church and Parish*, published by the then vicar, C.E. Matthews.

In 1925, one Lilian G. Thompson noticed, as she said, the name of the infant "Augustine Gobbo" amongst the entries for 1625, and wrote a letter announcing the discovery to the *Times Literary Supplement*. This was a very odd mistake: not only was Augustine Gobbo a misreading for Augustine Hobbs, but the entry of her christening is from 1593, not 1625. Circumstances strongly suggest that Lilian Thompson was writing from hearsay. But it was probably from this T.L.S. letter that the story crept into reputable text books; for instance into Harley Granville-Barker and G.B. Harrison's *A Companion to Shakespeare Studies* (1934) and ultimately into A.L. Rowse's *Shakespeare's Southampton* (1965). Matthews' successor G.S. Morley, an enthusiastic educationalist and historian, was meanwhile rewriting and extending the parish guide, and this edition, published in 1934, contained the 1593 'Gobbo' entry and two others - William 'Gobbo' married in 1667, and Thomas son of Thomas 'Gobbo' baptised in 1645; both the latter entries are in fact misreadings for 'Holte'. A few years later, Morley repeated this story to Arthur Mee, and indeed showed him the parish entries: Mee then published the mistaken entries in his often-reprinted and widely read *Hampshire and the Isle of Wight* (1939). It was probably via Mee that the story became 'oral tradition' in the Titchfield area.

It was not until 1968 that the Canadian scholar G.P.V. Akrigg, in his *Shakespeare and the Earl of Southampton* reported the misreadings, and those of us who are at present transcribing the Titchfield registers can confirm his judgements; although Hobbs and Holte are Titchfield family names, certainly no Gobbos ever existed in Titchfield.

Morely also recorded in his parish guide the 'incontrovertible fact' that the family of Shakespeare's 'great friend and fellow actor' William Beeston lived in Titchfield. The actor who for a time (about 1598) was in the Lord Chamberlain's company was in fact Christopher Beeston. He had a son William, who knew John Aubrey of the *Brief Lives* and died in London in 1682, but there is no evidence that this Beeston family had any connection with a family of some standing who lived at Posbrook in Titchfield in the 1630's. Of that family, the elder William Beeston was buried at Titchfield in 1638: his first son Henry became 'master of Winchester School', as he is described in the parish register: and his second son William, after becoming Lieutenant-Governor of Jamaica, was buried beneath a ledger stone in Titchfield Church in 1702.

So at least two stories connecting Shakespeare to Titchfield prove to be illusory. Akrigg, however, provides us with a reassuring piece of presumptive evidence. He points out that an eighteenth century plan of Place House marks a 'play-house room' on the now demolished second floor; and it does seem very likely that Shakespeare would have performed there for his patron the third Earl. That is all we can say. Some of the village traditions may be true, and in any case are very pleasant legends, so we are proposing a new one here. Wasn't Titchfield, where the cemetery lies next to the tanyard, the place where Shakespeare met that gravedigger in 'Hamlet' who was so expert on the durability of tanners?

The Map of 1610

In the last years of the Delmé estate, a large map, 6ft 9ins wide and 4ft 8ins in height, hung on the wall of the billiard room at Cams Hall. It was a map or plan of most of Titchfield parish, on a scale of about 1 foot to 1 mile, drawn (and originally coloured) at some time between 1605 and 1611. At the sale of the contents of Cams Hall in 1894, it was taken away by the then steward of the Delmé estates, but the Reverend G.A. Minns far sightedly had a tracing and copy made. Minns published this copy, in a much reduced form, in the Hampshire Field Club *Proceedings* of 1906, and a section showing Place House on what appears to be the original scale was printed both in the *Victoria County History* and in Field Club *Proceedings* of 1904. The map itself has since disappeared. Its discovery or even that of the original full-size copy would be of tremendous value to further historical studies of the area, for many details of buildings and even writing are too small and cramped to be clearly seen on Minns' still invaluable reproduction (the Place House section shows the kind of detail missing elsewhere). For instance, Minns marked on the reproduction, and explained, 79 of the place and field names from the original, but he did not explain some obscure words which we would very much like to read; and of course we cannot in any case be sure that the copyist actually bothered to transcribe everything he saw.

The map may well originally have been drawn as part of a survey in preparation for shutting off the haven. It provides us with our only detailed picture of the original estuary. Sailing craft are shown beached both on the east and the west of its mouth; another masted boat is shown at what was presumably a low-tide wharf between Little Posbrook and Hob Mill near Crofton; and two or three craft, gaily flying flags (pennants of the Earl of Southampton?) are shown at the high-tide wharf below Varman's Bridge near Hollam Farm. The only recently built iron mill is marked and named, and the village corn-mill with its wheel clearly shown. The parish church and village itself are frustratingly blurred in the reproduction, but some sixty houses and cottages are marked, many of them set apparently at right angles to the road line rather than parallel to it.

The Earl's interest in hunting and other sports is very apparent. The 'dog kennel' and 'dog house' were at what is now Carron Row Farm immediately north of the abbey site. Horsemen with lances are shown pursuing deer through the park north of Place House (here called The Place). A man in contemporary dress holding what looks like a fishing rod (though it may be a firearm) is shown standing near Hook Pond. Hounds, deer and what seem to be boar are drawn in all parts of the park north and west of Place House. The arable land is shown divided, as nowadays, into

51

many hedged fields; all but small patches of the former medieval open fields had long since been enclosed. The common grazing land west of the park, here called Swanwick Heath, is clearly marked, and of course remained common until 1866.

A number of names occur which have since been lost. The farm or group of buildings at Meon Marsh, for instance, was called Rithouse; an area of common land along Brownwich Lane was called Gibbinges Heath; and a building across the main road from the present Plessey site was called Fodda Howse. A striking feature of the map is the then large size of the hamlet at Meon; some 14 houses or cottages are marked where now there are four - this small community seems to have suffered from the closing of the estuary a year or two later. In spite of the copying problem, some features still appear on the map in surprising detail: the square enclosure of the village pound at the junction of Brownwich Lane and Common Lane, for instance; or what looks very much like a ducking stool at the riverside where the Fisherman's Rest now stands. We are given the approximate date of the map by the phrase: 'this copps felled Anno D 1605'; and the builder of the canal was not a Dutchman as legend has it, but presumably the Talbot who occupied the Talbots Wood which looked down on Varman's Bridge from Hollam Hill. One detail which we would dearly like to elucidate on the copy is the site of the Market Hall - if it was really already built. And if we had the original map would we be able to see the village cross which stood, we know, in the middle of the town in the fifteenth century, but at some time totally disappeared? Did the Market Hall replace the cross?

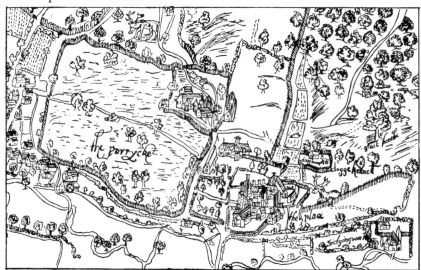

Part of the 1610 Map

52

The Market Hall

The Titchfield Market Hall which once stood in the centre of Titchfield Square is now part of the Weald and Downland Open Air Museum, just north of Chichester in West Sussex. Then in a state of disrepair and in danger of complete decay, it was dismantled in 1971, re-erected at Singleton in 1972, and restored to its original appearance.

The Market Hall may well have been originally built about 1612 at the expense of the third Earl as part of his development programme in those years. As we have seen it cannot be clearly distinguished on the 1610 map. The hall consisted of a ground floor with an open arcade within which market traders could lay out goods sheltered from the weather; and an upper floor with a meeting room and a small open gallery from which, no doubt, the Town Crier could read notices. The upper room was used for meetings of manorial and leet courts and other public meetings. The Titchfield Hall was constructed from a timber framework filled with close stud timber and herring-bone brickwork. Such timber market halls were once quite common in English towns, but have rarely survived. Many were rebuilt of stone or brick in the eighteenth and nineteenth centuries.

Dismantling the Market Hall

In his poem of 1740 Missing says that the market hall was then disused ('the Place for that erected stands unoccupy'd'); but it was still clearly marked, in its original position, on the Delmé estate map of 1753. We can guess that it was moved in or about 1810, when the Turnpike Trust obtained powers to repair the highway, to the position in Barry's Yard (behind the Queen's Head Hotel) now occupied by the surgery. At some point, perhaps about 1830, a cell or lock-up was built into the lower floor. Various changes were made to the walls over the years, and the roof line became half-hipped. The building in living memory was no more than a derelict shed partly covered with ivy. We must be grateful to the Singleton Museum and the Minet Trust for saving the building; but it is still a pity that the people of Titchfield have to travel to Sussex to see one of their historic heirlooms. We must hope some future generation will build a replica in Titchfield again for use as a small museum and information office.

St. Margaret's

The house called St. Margaret's, later St. Margaret's Priory, stands in wooded grounds off St. Margaret's Lane, near the source of the stream which runs through Barry's Meadow and under the High Street. It consists of an attractive Tudor House with a substantial late Georgian addition. The local tradition associating the construction of the house with the Armada and the threat of Spanish invasion may be accurate: the small brick tower, in good visibility, provides an excellent view of the former estuary and its approaches from Spithead. Another local tradition, that it was built as a dower-house for one of the Wriothesley ladies, cannot be confirmed - it may have been intended for a steward or other senior officer of the Wriothesley household - but several Delmé ladies certainly later lived there. The footpath from St. Margaret's through the strip of woodland called Slaughterhouse Copse to Fernhill Farm and Place House is known as the Ladies' Walk. This had evidently once been a footpath through the house site, because an undated manuscript among the Wriothesley papers records the agreement of the villagers to its re-routing along the side of the house. The footpath, and the house with its tower, outbuildings and grounds are clearly shown and named on the 1610 Map.

From the 1620's it seems no longer to have been used by the Wriothesley household: in 1641 it was described as a "capital messuage and farm called St. Margaret's, with a parcel of land enclosed from the great waste of Titchfield and two closes called Low Lamberts and the Outash". A century later Missing referred to it as "a farmer's dwelling now tho' then a Lord's", and the 1753 Survey called it St. Margaret's Farm. In the late eighteenth century the new lords of the manor, the Delmés, brought the house back into use for members of the family. On the break up of the Delmé estate, the house was bought in 1919 by Gore Hughes-Stanton, an enthusiastic artist and antiquarian, who in fact added many of the "Tudor" features which we see today (he did the same thing at the Old Lodge in East Street). The romantic but unhistoric name Priory was added later and a short time after the last representative of the Parry family died in 1948, the house was divided into three.

The Canal

The most ambitious of the third Earl's projects for the development of his estates was the closing of the Meon estuary and the replacement of the navigable tidal channel by a canal. This canal, once called the New River and in recent times just "the river", runs to the west of the old winding channel from just below the Titchfield corn mill past the parish church and Great Posbrook to the sea near Meon beach. Visitors can follow the towpath from the footbridge behind the parish church to the former sea-lock at Meon Bridge.

The works were completed in 1611. In that year the parish register noted on 23rd June that "Titchfield Haven was shut out by one Richard Talbottes industry under God's permission at the cost of the Right Honourable the Earle of Southampton". Village legend has it that Dutch engineers were hired for the undertaking. This may well be true, but the Talbots were a local family, and no Dutch names appear in the parish registers.

A shingle bank was built across most of the mouth of the estuary but leaving two exits. One, to the east, was controlled by a large sluice gate which regulated the flow of water from the enclosed and now fresh water Haven into the small harbour at Hill Head. The other, to the west, originally permitted the tide to flow into a small inlet and up to a point below Meon hamlet where a sea-lock was built (SU532027). The remains of this lock suggest that it was a "staunch" lock, with a single pair of gates. Vessels passing back and forth would have waited until the tide reached the water level in the canal, when the gates would have been opened; the lock could not therefore, like more modern locks, have been used at all states of the tide.

The Canal

We are still uncertain about the main purpose of the whole project: remarkably few documents exist which tell us anything about it. There is no doubt that it was at least in part a water-meadow system. Water-meadows - the controlled flooding or irrigation of meadows for the production of more hay and grass - were a continental development and in 1611 only a recent introduction into England. A regular series of small sluice gates along the canal, most of them destroyed in living memory, permitted the water in the canal to be used in this way; White's Directory in 1859 in fact says that the canal was "chiefly for the purpose of drainage and irrigation, and not now used for the navigation of barges". Presumably it was intended that with increased fodder the whole estate would carry a larger number of cattle and sheep, providing meat, hides and wool.

On the other hand, the third Earl, as we have seen, was also interested in shipping. He was a very active sponsor of the exploration and development of North America; closer to home his enthusiasm was once illustrated by his advice to a friend that Titchfield was the best place on the mainland from which to take a ferry to the Isle of Wight; and it is inconceivable that he would have willingly given up the capacity which even the muddy old channel had provided of bringing heavy goods up to Titchfield. Indeed, the siting of the canal, with its broad, fairly straight channel leading up to just below the corn mill (grain, flour), next to the tannery (lime, hides, leather), past the church (stone) and with a bridle path to the market square (wool) is too deliberate to be an accident.

But there is a third possible motive for the project. The Earl and his friends were very enthusiastic sportsmen - fishing, shooting and hunting animals of all kinds. The newly enclosed area around the Haven was, as it still is, rich in wild life, and it is not impossible that this wealthy and still fairly young man was deliberately creating an expensive playground.

Indeed it may be that the intended multiple uses of this project were one reason for its failure: it is possible that neither the navigation nor the irrigation were efficient enough to make the expensive maintenance of the lock and the sluices (and perhaps at first a swing-bridge on the Crofton road) worthwhile.

Inevitably too the Earl and his successors had to contend with the forces of nature - floods, high tides, currents and storms. A map in the Hampshire Record Office, undated but apparently from about 1750, makes it clear that sometime in the early eighteenth century the original shingle bank had been destroyed by the sea and a second bank had to be built (the bank on which the beach huts now stand) about two hundred yards seaward of the first, and a new sluice constructed to drain the Haven about a hundred yards inland from the original sluice (parts of which can still be seen). The upkeep of the whole system was obviously an endless drain on the estate's resources.

At the same time the value of the trade in and out of Titchfield declined as from 1650 to 1750 the little town went through perhaps the lowest point in its prosperity. Eighteenth century maps show us that a permanent bridge was built at the end of Bridge Street, and farm bridges near Great and Little Posbrook, which would have made navigation difficult if not quite impossible. More important the width of the lock at Meon was filled by two small arches and the whole structure changed into a bridge, still indeed the present Meon Road bridge. The old lock gates remained only as sluice gates.

Hammond's Bridge near Little Posbrook

Further works took place in the early nineteenth century, the brick bridge carrying the turnpike being built across the head of the canal below the mill, and the farm bridges near Great and Little Posbrook being replaced by twin-arched brick bridges. The little tidal inlet which had once carried boats up to the lock still remained, and Ordnance Survey maps of the mid-nineteenth century still mark the old lock as "Highest Point to which Ordinary Tides flow". But the diaries of James Hewett of Posbrook (now in the Portsmouth Records Office) show that in the 1870's its mouth was being closed by shingle drift. Hewett in fact obtained Board of Trade permission to dig a new outlet to "Posbrook Haven" but his efforts evidently failed. "Posbrook Haven" is now the area of stagnant water and reeds immediately behind the beach huts. In the 1890's a new brick sluice was constructed above the lock to carry the water from the canal into the main Haven and thence into the sea at Hill Head.

Those visitors to the site, however, who look beyond the modern tarmac can still see the masonry of the Earl's original lock, its stone almost certainly taken from demolished abbey buildings and its method of construction very similar to that of its contemporary, Stony Bridge near the abbey. This may have been a relatively small and ultimately unsuccessful project; but it was fifty years earlier than the Itchen Navigation and 150 years earlier than the Duke of Bridgewater's famous canal at Manchester.

Medieval Fishponds

The medieval fishponds west of Place House are well known and easily seen from the footpath leading off the track to Fernhill Farm and the ancient barn or by visiting the small private museum at Carron Row. But until recently a much larger set of medieval fishponds remained difficult to see and almost unknown. The construction of a new road (1981) running westwards from the end of St. Margaret's Lane has now made it possible to see the whole range of these ponds.

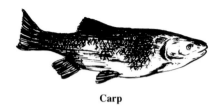

Carp

A small stream, formerly called the Brownwich Brook, runs parallel to the river Meon about a mile to the west, rising near the M27 and running south to the Solent at Brownwich. It runs beneath the A27 just west of the Plessey/Census Office site; beneath the new road just above the historic Pest House; and beneath the Titchfield-Warsash road at 'the Sluice'. The stream was crossed at various points by the now disturbed remains of substantial banks which were the retaining banks of five large ponds each from 300 to 700 metres in length. We do not know the name of the northern pond, but the lower four were called Lamberts, Hook, Hunt and Holme ponds. The three modern roads run on the line of three of the original banks, though these are partially buried under the modern embankments. The A27, at what is traditionally called Three Stone Bottom (SU527071) follows an S-bend over the stream, with a former pond lying to the north between the main road and Titchfield Park Road. The new road also snakes across the stream (SU528063), leaving the medieval bank partly undisturbed on its north side. This is a good point from which to see the pond system, particularly in the winter and after heavy rain - the silted up bed of Hunt's Pond lies below the embankment, and Hook Pond, now grown in by trees and bushes, above it. The one bank not used by a modern road (SU528066) can be seen from the new road crossing the valley on a line with the main Plessey building. On the Warsash road, the modern road curves awkwardly over the stream with the lower end of Hunt's Pond lying in the woodland called The Wilderness to the north. Further southwards, in undergrowth, are the banks of Holmepond, dug out again to form a pond in the dry summer of 1976 (SU524049).

The Brownwich Brook, for part of its course, formed the boundary between the cultivated fields of Titchfield and its common - Titchfield Common, Swanwick Heath or Locks Heath - until the enclosure of 1859-66. The ponds there date from the thirteenth or fourteenth centuries.

The valuation ('extent') of the Abbey's manors in 1381 refers to six fishponds - two of them 'within the abbey' (no doubt the lower two ponds at Carron Row), one 'in the park' (possibly the pond at Titchfield Park Road), and three 'on the rector's moor' (probably Lambert's, Hook and Hunt's ponds).

Lambert's Pond was mentioned by name in the 1381 extent. Hunt Pond was named in 1393 when Richard II rode from Warsash to Titchfield via the south end of this pond: this was the notorious occasion when some of the king's baggage was lost in the other pond, east of the Jolly Farmer inn at Fleet End, which fed the medieval mill there.

After the dissolution, the first Earl of Southampton restocked two fishponds at the abbey, and another four fishponds 'a mile in length', presumably four of the ponds along the Brownwich Brook. A year or two later the traveller Leland, also on his way from Warsash, 'left a pretty lake on the left a little ere I entered into Titchfield town' - probably Hunt Pond. Two of the Brownwich Brook ponds, Hunt and Hook Ponds, are named on the 1610 map.

Most of the ponds were allowed to decay in the early 18th century. But at the end of the 19th century Hunt Pond was dug out again and turned into an ornamental lake in the grounds of West Hill Park. After the enclosure of Titchfield Common, this pond gave its name to Hunt's Pond Road. In recent years the pond has again silted up.

Overlooking Lambert's Pond from the north, and between the pond and the (A27) road was a site surrounded by a circle of trees and described on 18th century maps as the Bowling Green (across the road from the Plessey site). Various ditches and banks apparently connected with these features survive in the tangled woodland, though they have been badly disturbed by gravel digging (SU528069). It is clear that a number of sporting activities took place on this site. The three large stones which once stood at Three Stone Bottom and which were the subject of village superstitions were buried during modern roadworks. They were presumably sarsens unearthed, perhaps, when the fishponds were dug. Three large unweathered sarsens have been found on the line of the new road near Hook Pond. Sarsens seem to lie only a few feet under the silt all the way along the valley bottom here. The Society would like to see some of these recovered and made into a village feature before they disappear forever.

Mills

Mills on the River Meon

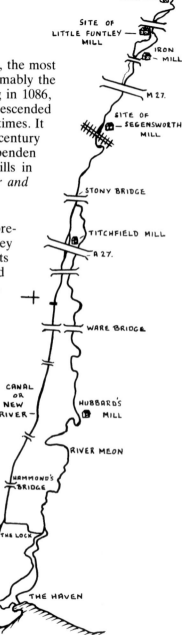

Great Funtley Mill (SU556090). This mill, the most northerly in the ancient parish was presumably the mill on Ranulf Flamme's Funtley holding in 1086, worth 12s. 6d (60½p), and its ownership descended with the Great Funtley estate until recent times. It was a corn mill until the early twentieth century and was formerly occupied by the Tappenden family, who still run the Chesapeake Mills in Wickham. The site is described in *Water and Wind Mills in Hampshire*.

Little Funtley Mill (SU553087). This was presumably the mill on Count Alan's Funtley holding in 1086, worth 10s. (50p) and its ownership descended with the estate called at different times Funtley Furstbury, Funtley Pagham and Little Funtley until the seventeenth century. The mill lay immediately to the south of Longwater Bridge; its pond, or wide head-leat, immediately north of the bridge, still exists. The mill site itself can no longer be seen on the ground, but is visible in air photographs. By 1350 the mill, then in the hands of Thomas le Wayte of Funtley Furstbury, was a fulling-mill, and its continued use for fulling cloth until the sixteenth century is suggested by John Wayte of Segensworth's occupation of wool merchant in 1527.

It is possible that the construction in 1603 of the pond and head-leat of the Iron Mill further downstream made Little Funtley unusable; at all events it is marked as "Old Mill" on the 1610 map. The site does not seem to have been worked as a mill in the eighteenth century, although it was still called Little Mill in 1803. The buildings disappeared soon afterwards.

Titchfield (or Funtley) Iron Mill (SU550082). This mill seems to have been built on a virgin site by the third Earl of Southampton in 1603-5; it was marked as "Iron Myll" on the 1610 Map. Its construction seems to have been one of the projects by which the Earl hoped to restore his fortunes after his release from the Tower. The site is discussed in *Water and Wind Mills in Hampshire* and in *Hampshire Industrial Archaeology*. Its history is described more fully below.

Segensworth Mill (SU542071). There was a mill on Hugh de Port's estate at Segensworth in 1086, worth 20s., but it seems to have fallen into disrepair before 1350 since it is not mentioned in a dispute of that year between Thomas le Wayte and the Abbot of Titchfield about the effect of the tail-leat of Little Funtley Mill on the Abbot's meadows. The site cannot be identified and was perhaps obliterated by the construction of the present railway embankment.

Titchfield Corn Mill

Titchfield Mill (SU542061). The village corn-mill at Titchfield is probably of great antiquity. Its site would seem to be the only possible location for the "King's Mill", and "mill-dyke" of which, presumably the head-leat, is mentioned in the bounds of a meadow at Segensworth in 982 A.D.

Titchfield was, of course, a royal manor, part of the estates of Edward the Confessor before the Norman Conquest. The mill was mentioned in Domesday Book in 1086, worth 20s. In the Middle Ages it appears frequently in the records of Titchfield Abbey, though it in fact formed part of the small estate then held in Titchfield by the nuns of St. Elizabeth, Winchester. The buildings and a wheel are shown very clearly in the 1610 map. The present building with its two iron wheels dates from 1830, and incorporates stone from the Place House site in its foundation. The mill was sold during the break-up of the Delmé estate in 1919, and was bought by the Titchfield Abbey Co-operative Society, which, as Titchfield Mills Ltd., continues to sell feedstuffs and other agricultural requisites. Milling was discontinued in the 1950's, but the stones and other machinery are still in place. The mill is described in *Water and Wind Mills in Hampshire.*

Hubbard's Mill (SU543042). This was probably the mill on Count Alan's estate in Crofton in 1086, worth 12s. 6d (60½p). Crofton Mill appears frequently in the medieval records of Titchfield Abbey: for instance, certain tenants were required to take their corn to Crofton Mill. The buildings are marked, though not named, on the 1610 map, and the mill itself is shown on a number of eighteenth and nineteenth century maps, variously called Hubbards, Hob, Hobboday and Hubbardsmiths Mill (this last name may indicate that at some point metal-working took place on the site). The site seems to have been only a farm in the nineteenth century, when all trace of the mill had disappeared. The site's long history however makes very unlikely the suggestions in *Water and Wind Mills of Hampshire* that there never had been a mill here. The closing of the tidal estuary in 1611 may have totally altered the environs of this, the lowest mill on the Meon. It is not clear whether the mill was powered by a leat from the main stream; by the tide; or by the rivulet which runs westwards from Crofton into the Meon.

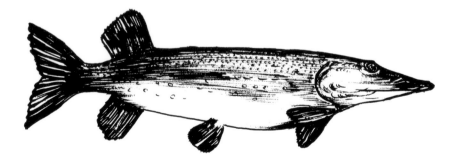

Pike

Water Mill on Titchfield Common

In the fourteenth century Titchfield Abbey built a water-mill at Fleet end on the western edge of Titchfield Common, below the huge dam of its fishpond there, now long disused. The rectangular site of the mill can still be discerned in the woodland next to the footpath (SU509059). The mill soon fell into disrepair, probably as a result of the Black Death.

Other Mills

There were at least two windmills in Titchfield parish in the late eighteenth century: a windmill at Peel Common east of Crofton and another on Titchfield Common near the present Sir Joseph Paxton public house. The windmill on the Common disappeared in the nineteenth century, perhaps as a result of the enclosure; but the tower on Peel Common was still standing in the 1920's. Water-driven farm machinery of the nineteenth century has recently been identified at Brownwich Farm.

Peel Common Windmill

Historic Bridges over the River Meon

Stony Bridge or "Anjou" Bridge (SU554066). The original bridge at this point may date from the construction of the abbey in 1232. It is first mentioned in the late fourteenth century, when it was called Kettelbridge, perhaps from the swirling waters beneath it during floods. It seems at that time to have been a wooden bridge with stone piers, because when on one occasion it was damaged by floods, the river could still be crossed by jumping from stone to stone. In 1372 a citizen of Southampton, one Thomas Harpeter, paid for the construction of a new section of wooden causeway leading to the bridge and the bridge was still made of wood when Leland crossed it in 1542. There seems no reason to doubt the local tradition that the date "1625" was once visible on the present stone structure, its planning would thus have been part of the third Earl's energetic estate development. The traditional association of its construction with the marriage of Henry VI and Margaret of Anjou in 1445 would seem to be only a legend, though no doubt their party crossed the wooden bridge on their way from Southwick Priory to the abbey to continue their wedding celebrations.

Warebridge or Waremonnesbridge (SU542055). This bridge, built at the former high point of normal tides and carrying the road to Hollam and Crofton, is almost certainly the oldest in Titchfield. Its name is probably derived from the medieval word for seaweed - "wara". It was mentioned in the fourteenth century during a dispute over its upkeep. Leland in 1542 called it Warebridge and said it was built of timber. The 1610 map calls it Varmans Bridge, and shows small masted ships in the pool below the bridge which was the "port" of Titchfield until the closing of the estuary. After the construction of the canal, Warebridge became one of the pair of bridges on the road to Crofton, and is now hardly recognisable under the road.

Hammonds Bridge (SU539049) is one of the twin-arched brick bridges built in the early nineteenth century, replacing eighteenth century bridges built when the canal became disused. It joins Little Posbrook and Meon hamlet to the water-meadows. Its name was taken from the Hammonds Meadow and Hammonds Coppice nearby. These simple facts did not prevent Edwardian antiquarians from associating the bridge with Colonel Hammond and inventing the legend that Charles I was arrested in 1647 while trying to hide under a bridge which was not then in existence!

Stony or Anjou Bridge

Titchfield (or Funtley) Iron-Mill

Iron-making at Titchfield dates from the turn of the seventeenth century when the third Earl began to restore the fortunes of his estates; the water-powered forge on the Meon was built in 1603-5. By 1605 iron-working at Beaulieu and Titchfield had become a joint operation, iron-stone being collected at Hengistbury Head and smelted at Sowley blast-furnace near Lymington (SU378964). The resulting pig-iron was shipped to Titchfield forge to be converted into wrought-iron, the Meon providing a more reliable source of power for the forge-hammers than the Sowley pond. The finished bar-iron may well have been used in the local ship-building industry, or may even have been shipped to Virginia. There is evidence to suggest that by 1623 the first tin-plate mill in England had been established at Titchfield, the Earl having put up £1,000 in partnership with two London girdlers to produce "Crooked Lane" ware - kitchen utensils which would have been made in the forge and dipped in tin. Although London was the main market for such items, it is possible that some tin plates were supplied to Portsmouth Dockyard. By 1628 a second plate-mill was in operation at Wickham under the ownership of Sir William Uvedale. This was assigned to the Earl in 1647, to be run by John Gringo, who was also involved in working Titchfield Mill. The fourth Earl successfully blocked attempts by others to secure patents for tin-plating, but the apparent cessation of activities after this Earl's death in 1667 suggests that tin-plating had never been very profitable.

From 1647 to 1773 the mill appears to have been run by the Gringos, whose activities provide an interesting insight into the careers of entrepreneurs at that time. They were a Quaker family, one branch being buried in the Friends Burial Ground at Swanmore, another at Ringwood. Quakers were often associated with iron-working, and with the early stages of what we call the Industrial Revolution.

The output of Titchfield Mill in this period was in the region of 200 tons of wrought iron per annum, which would have required approximately 1.1 million cubic feet of cordwood from local coppices to provide charcoal fuel. The Gringos owned coppices in the Fawley area, no doubt supplying fuel to Sowley blast furnace, with which they were connected until the early 1700's. In addition to operating the Wickham and Titchfield forges, the Gringos constructed a blast-furnace at Bursledon, that may have supplied Titchfield forge by way of Fareham Quay, which they also built. On the death of the last of the Gringos (John) c.1776, the quay passed into the hands of Peter Barfoot.

The iron-mill is best known for the activities of Henry Cort (1740-1800), who took over the mill in 1775. Cort's patents for puddling iron with raw pit coal in a reverberatory furnace and for rolling iron bar by means of grooved rollers (1783 and 1784) allowed the integration of iron-making processes on the coal-fields, and provided a cheaper source of good wrought iron than the imports from Sweden and Russia on which England had previously relied. Cort was able to convert old dockyard iron into good new iron, shipments to his Gosport works or from the yard arriving via Fareham Creek, Cort having rented Barfoot's Quay for £25 per annum.

The life and work of Cort have been well documented, but little has been known of the actual forge arrangements. Recent excavations have provided evidence of a single reverberatory furnace, which would have been worked in conjunction with a refinery forge, at one end of the site, while at the other end is the probable location of a pair of tilt-hammers. The rollers would have been driven by two parallel shafts, rotating in the same direction, each with its own fly-wheel. A description of the site in 1806 allows a calculation that iron could be processed through the rollers at a rate of 2ft. per second, which must have been a tricky operation in such a confined area. There is no evidence of a blast-furnace or furnace slag, though a small foundry was in operation by 1784, Cort and his partner Samuel Jellicoe supplying £39 worth of cast-iron weights for the new turnpike weighing-machine at Fareham in that year. A second, much smaller water-wheel on the site probably provided power for the bellows in the smithy, which adjoined the forge; the surviving part of this building is shown as a coal-store by the 1830's.

The Iron Mill in the eighteenth century

69

Following Cort's bankruptcy, and a period of tenure by Samuel Jellicoe during the profitable war period, the works were sold in 1815 to John Bartholemew, Cort's former finery-man. His son, James, initiated a period of experimental gunnery - percussion firing of large guns, trials with breach-loading cannon, and the making of shells which would "explode on striking a ship's side". This period of experiments - probably between 1836 and 1845 - seems to have impoverished the Bartholemews; though the mill is still found working on a small scale in 1864, it was probably closed after a disastrous fire in the 1880's.

The "little mill at Funtley" thus acquires some significance in the history of iron-making in this country. Of the four main phases of ownership, three are accompanied by technical innovation; tin-plating, puddling and rolling, naval gunnery - while the fourth, under the Gringos, provides a classic example of early vertical integration in the industry, no doubt stimulated by the growth of Portsmouth Dockyard.

The remains of the mill are still visible from the footpath through Fontley House Farm (SU550082), and the handsome Ironmaster's House is still in private occupation.

A Poem about Titchfield

Until recently few people were aware that there was in existence a long poem about Titchfield. Called "Titchfield: A Poetical Essay", it was written by John Missing, a member of a prominent local family of the time who lived at Crofton and Posbrook, and was published in 1749. Fairly modest as a piece of literature, we can assume that only a few copies of a single edition were published. Most of the poem recounts the melodramatic story of the lovers Eliza and Celadon, but the setting is Titchfield, and we are given interesting glimpses of the village in the 1740's. Place House, for instance, is described even at that time as in disrepair:

> ... *now its tottring Tow'rs are sunk in Dust*

St. Margaret's is mentioned:

> *A Farmer's Dwelling now tho' then a Lord's*

And the iron-mill:

> *Beneath their sturdy Blows the Anvils groan*

The author was clearly interested in fishing and wild-fowling: he mentions angling for trout, netting carp and shooting the cormorants which were destroying the eels. He gives us a glimpse of the cruel sport of otter-baiting: the otters were caught in gins and then:

> *... in Triumph, to the Village bear*
> *The hostile Animal: there let the Dogs*
> *The rav'ning Traitor bait ...*

Missing gives a picture of the village at a low point in its fortunes

> *Next on the Village cast your Eyes, where high*
> *In Air the lofty Maypole rears its Head ...*
> *Then view the empty Market, how the Place*
> *for that erected stands unoccupyd;*
> *In Times of old 'tis said, the Town enjoy'd*
> *Some Commerce; but it now neglected lies,*
> *And Husbandry alone the Folk employs.*
> *Here Silence reigns, unless when rural Sports*
> *Call forth the rosy Youth; and Jollity,*
> *and Gambols, reign around ...*

In fact, the population of the parish was already beginning to rise again at the time Missing was writing. The Society hopes to publish a new edition of the poem in the near future.

Titchfield in the Eighteenth Century

The existence of parish registers for Titchfield provides us from 1589 onwards with a new source with which to study the population and other aspects of the history of the village. The numbers of tenants in the abbey's rental of 1377 suggest a total population in the parish at that time of about 1,500 people; the Wriothesley rental of 1546 indicates a considerable decline, to perhaps 1,000 people at the dissolution. By the end of the sixteenth century the parish registers allow us to calculate the population in a different way, from the numbers of christenings, burials and marriages: they suggest a population of about 1,200 in 1600 and a steady increase during the beneficent management of the third Earl of Southampton and indeed on to a high point of perhaps 1,800 people in the early 1640's at the beginning of the Civil War. Thereafter, for still obscure reasons, there seems to have been an irregular but ultimately sharp decline to another low point of only 1,000 about 1720. That was the point of depression at which the canal seems to have become disused, and which Missing recalled in his poem, but the parish registers show us that by 1740 the population and with it the prosperity of the village had begun to revive. The population in fact increased very rapidly throughout the latter part of the eighteenth century almost trebling to 2,949 by the first Census of 1801.

At the same time the ordinary people of the parish took an increasing part in managing their own affairs. After the death of the third Earl the local landowners, whether Wriothesley descendents or Delmé, became more and more remote from the day-to-day events in the village. The manorial court and the reeves and other officers appointed there disappeared and the lord's "court baron" became a mere formality (perhaps that is why the upper room of the Market Hall became disused). Their place was taken by the parishioners meeting in the church vestry, and the officers - the overseers of the poor, the overseers of the highways, and others - that they appointed. The accumulated bulk of the minutes of their meetings and other papers now in the County Records Office at Winchester are witness to the increasing complexity of the expanding English society of the eighteenth century, even in Titchfield.

A major problem for the parish was the growing number of poor people within the rising population. In 1701 the poor rate was 4s. (20p) to the yardland (the yardland, the old virgate, was now only a notional unit of rating and in fact was discarded a few years later in favour of the more recent valuation system). By 1711 the rate was 20s. (£1) to the yardland, and by 1714, in the depths of the depression of those years, 25s. The parish continued to raise heavy poor rates throughout the century, sometimes needing two or even three supplementary rates during the year! In 1732 it

The Watchman

was decided that it would be cheaper to put poor people into a workhouse than to give them payments to live outside. A large house, with a coach-house, other outbuildings, an orchard and garden in Mill Street was bought for conversion to a workhouse, and the first Master and Mistress of the Workhouse appointed. A parish doctor (from 1715) was already being employed to care for the sick poor. But the workhouse and the problems of poverty and disease continued to pose problems for the ratepayers. The coach-house was converted into an isolation ward in 1749, but proved inadequate: so in 1753 a really isolated building, what seems to have been an old gamekeeper's house near Hook Pond, now known as Earl's Charity, was acquired as a pest-house. An extension was built on to the workhouse in 1762 and more alterations done in 1771. However, like most other English parishes, Titchfield failed to solve the problem of the poor at this time and was finally reluctantly forced to surrender its responsibilities to the Poor Law Union, with its workhouse at Fareham, in the 1830's. In the same way, the parish failed to cope with the maintenance of the highway, and had its powers over the main roads taken by the Turnpike Trust.

Another of the miniature welfare-state activities of the parish was fire-fighting: a horse-drawn fire-engine was bought by the parish in 1772 (the nineteenth century replacement for this can still be seen at Carron Row Farm), and another growing social problem was crime. It was by now of course the magistrates and the Quarter Sessions at Winchester who were primarily responsible for dealing with major crime. The parish became involved by offering rewards and undertaking prosecutions. In the 1760's, the village was plagued by a gang who were robbing travellers on the highway from Fareham. The gang turned out to be five Titchfield men led by a certain John Martin, a labourer. When identified, Martin fled to Surrey where he was caught, but afterwards released; he continued his life of crime and was arrested again in 1770. We do not as yet know what eventually happened to this local highwayman.

Titchfield was obviously a lively place in the 1740's and 1750's. As we have seen, Missing's poem has a number of references to field sports and a detailed map drawn for the Delmé family in 1753 gives us other evidence of the growing interest in sport. There was something like an unofficial sports centre at the edge of the common on both sides of Lambert's Pond, with a "course" for horse-races on the west side, and a circular "bowling-green" (which we guess was actually a cockpit - well away from the church and eye of the respectable inhabitants of the village) on the east side. There were two other bowling-greens in the village - one on the site of the present garden centre at Place House, another between the church and the vicarage. By the end of the century, cricket had appeared.

The 1753 Survey shows us that by that time the former open arable fields had virtually disappeared: only a few patches of land in which tenants held plots side-by-side remained - in the Garston, for instance, and at Stephanbridge. Otherwise the arable land of the parish was divided amongst eight or nine substantial farms west of the river and four or five east of the river. The larger village houses were now occupied not by small farmers as in the past, but by innkeepers like James Brown of The Bugle, tradespeople like Mrs. Moyle of the tanyard and moderately well-off residents often connected with the Navy. It was a pattern which was to continue into the present century. One difference to today is that the 1753 map shows the Market Hall standing right in the middle of the Square with several smaller buildings, presumably permanent stalls, standing around it. The market was then a regular Saturday market (it was later to change to Monday fortnights) and there were four fairs every year (later only two).

In the period of agricultural decline from about 1630 to 1730, the woodland in the parish had come to assume a greater importance in the local economy. The Admiralty contractors dealing with the fourth Earl in 1635 said that "the whole Kingdom could not better the thousand trees agreed for there". Another naval officer in 1668 thought that there was no better timber outside the New Forest: he regretted that some of it was, in his view, being wasted in making buckets. During the naval wars of the eighteenth century the woodland, particularly of Place House Park and of the old forest area in the north of the parish, continued to supply timber for building and ship-building; charcoal for iron-working; faggots for ovens; bark for tanning; hurdles; "withies"; and the many other wooden articles we have now replaced by plastic ones.

We are fortunate in having evidence, later in the eighteenth century, of the husbandry practised on one of the large farms. The famous agricultural writer, Arthur Young, published his *Annals of Agriculture,* correspondence between himself and go-ahead farmers from all parts of the country. Among these were two members of the Waller family who had a farm at Crofton. They describe the farms in the parish as very prosperous at this time, grubbing out woodland to create new arable fields: we can relate this prosperity to the rapidly growing population. The fields were manured both by carting seaweed and mud from the sea-shore (a medieval practice in Titchfield) and by bringing huge quantities of urban dung from the rapidly growing towns of Portsmouth and Gosport (which of course did not yet have sewerage systems). The products however were still strongly traditional, very similar to those of the medieval abbey - grain (wheat, barley, oats) and sheep, with clover, peas and vetches used in rotation. Root crops like turnips and potatoes and market garden crops like cabbages were still a novelty, and dairy farming of minor importance.

Although woodland was in places being cleared, the Wallers also comment on its value for timber and for coppice wood, both in great demand at this period. They refer approvingly too to one of the great users of coppice wood in the parish, Mr. Cort's very modern iron-works at Funtley! We can see that during the middle years of the eighteenth century, the years of Rule Britannia, Titchfield had developed a well-balanced relationship with the thriving naval towns of Portsmouth and Gosport, providing mutton, flour, timber and iron, and receiving in exchange cash and manure. It was a miniature economic system which was to disappear, or at least change, after Waterloo.

Drawing of the Market Square circa 1830

The Delmé Family

A large tombstone slab, just beside the path in the south-eastern part of the graveyard at Titchfield Church, marks the end of the dominance of the Delmé family within the district stretching from Cornaway Lane, Portchester to Brownwich Farm, Titchfield:

Delmé arms

Sacred to the memory of
Mary, the wife of Henry Peter Delmé Esq
of Cams Hall in this county
Also H P Delmé
Lord of the Manors of Titchfield, Segensworth, Crofton
Newlands, Lee Marks, Lee Britten, Chark, Mirabel and Cams Oysell
in the County of Hampshire and former High Sheriff of the county
who died at Cams Hall at the age of 89 years, in 1883
also Captain George Delmé
and of Frances Amelia Delmé
eldest daughter of the late John Delmé
also Jane Delmé
wife of Seymour Robert Delmé
and Seymour Robert Delmé
Lord of the Manors of ...
Died in March 1894. Aged 86 years

This may seem a gloomy way to begin a short account of the Delmés in Titchfield and Fareham; but the presence of the tomb shows their attachment to Titchfield even though their home had been at Cams Hall in Fareham for many years.

The Delmés were a Walloon family who came originally from the continent as a result of religious persecution, and became pastors of Walloon churches in Norwich, and later Canterbury and London. The Walloons had strong connections with Southampton, and we soon find a link between the Delmés and our own area.

In the seventeenth century, the third English generation furnished a pastor for the French church in London, and the third son, Pierre Delmé became a merchant and citizen of London. By his marriage to Sibella Nightingale he fathered a family of nine children, two of whom are buried in Southampton. His will shows him to have been a man of substance.

His third son, Peter, proceeded to build on this foundation. This first Peter married twice. His first wife, Anne Matcham, was the daughter of a Southampton grocer and Mayor, and mother of his surviving children. Peter himself became a London alderman, was knighted in 1714, became a governor of the Bank of England, and in 1723 Lord Mayor. On his death in 1728 his estate was worth £160,000 in cash alone, with many merchant ventures, and debts accruing, from Constantinople to Rio de Janeiro.

The next Peter, the eldest son of the first, came of age four years after his father's death, and inherited £300,000 through the death of his youngest brother Samuel. He too added to his wealth by marrying well: his first wife brought him an estate in Eltham in Kent, and his second wife Erlestoke in Wiltshire. In 1741 he was elected Member of Parliament for Southampton and gave the town £500 for its political discernment! Holy Rood Church there was given its eight bells at the same time, and Peter became a freeman of Southampton.

The second Peter's next purchase, in the same year, was the manor of Titchfield and Palace House. A patron of the arts and a connoisseur of books and sculpture, the Delmé family fortune seemed set to continue. But then came tragedy. The newspapers of 1770 record the death of Peter Delmé Esquire of an apoplectic fit! Peter had in fact shot himself. He was buried in the family vault in London. His will refers to numerous charities in all his estates, including £20 to the poor of Titchfield, and annuities to old servants in the area. As he had the living of Titchfield Church, he tried to keep that living in the hands of his godson's father, so that his godson, Peter Taylor, could succeed when of age! In fact he never did, though we do not know why.

A year before his father's death, the next Peter Delmé - the third of that name - seemed to have cemented the family fortunes by marrying into the aristocracy. He married Lady Elizabeth Howard, daughter of the Earl of Carlisle, a "beauty of the court" who was later painted by Reynolds, but Peter began a rake's progress, and his wealth rapidly disappeared. At this time the family were frequently at Titchfield, their domestic parson came from the village, and they lived at the Palace House. But - according to local legend - as a result of a fire at the Palace House, the Delmés sought a new mansion in Cams Hall near Fareham. At first they could not raise the £18,000 which was asked for it. The third Peter died in 1780, at the age of 41, leaving his wife Lady Betty with the problem. She proved equal to the task, backed by her family, the Carlisles.

All the rents of the family's properties in London, Erlestoke and Titchfield were raised; she refused the full amount granted to her by her husband in the marriage settlement; and she sold off unwanted houses in Southampton - so Cams Hall was acquired. The whole of Titchfield manor was resurveyed, East Cams Farm was purchased, her son John was married off as a minor to Frances Garnier of Rookesbury, and by the time he came of age the lands were clear of debt, and the money was available to enlarge and alter Cams Hall. During the enlargement of Cams much material was taken from Place House (as it was now called) - stone masonry, bricks and timbers - which can be seen to this day in the old stables and orangery. Lady Betty herself remarried, into the same Garnier family, only to be widowed again two years later. She finally retired to St. Margaret's.

John died at the early age of 36 leaving a family of seven boys and four girls. He died before his plans for the enlargement of Cams Hall could be completed, but he had again consolidated the family lands and fortune. On his death, in 1809, John was buried in Titchfield Church, in a vault close to the altar. His eldest son, a second John, lived only to 1815, dying suddenly at the age of 23 years. He too was buried in Titchfield Church. Like all his family, he had made generous gifts to charities and to the poor of the parishes around. His mother outlived him, residing like her predecessor at St. Margaret's until her death.

Delmé memorial

Henry Peter Delmé, another of the seven sons of John, succeeded to the estates and unlike his father and brother enjoyed them for nearly 70 years. All the estates were resurveyed, and improved farming practices and husbandry were encouraged; during this period the first railway was constructed through Fareham, and Titchfield Common was enclosed. Henry Peter was generous in giving money for the building of churches and schools and for many charities. When he died in 1883 at the age of 89, he left instructions for a private funeral at Titchfield, but many of his tenants attended the funeral as a mark of respect.

Henry Peter was succeeded by his brother, Seymour Robert Delmé, a man already by then 70 and the last of the male heirs. Something of an eccentric and a recluse, he too did much charitable good in schools and churches of the area. However he resisted the proposal for the railway to go through Titchfield. He objected because it 'would so sever his land in such a way as to interfere with its enjoyment ... and further objects to the proposal as it would be necessary to erect a viaduct at Segensworth'. Being remarkably fair-minded, when he heard that the villagers at Titchfield were in favour of a railway, but did not have enough money to fight their case, he made a large donation to their cause. A few years later the viaduct at Segensworth was erected and the vital station at Swanwick opened.

On his death the lands were willed away. All the property was sold and the money, apart from large gifts to charities, went to his married nieces. A great nephew, Charles, reacquired the Titchfield property for a short time but he resold it before emigrating to Western Canada.

So we come to the end of a great family, which held sway for over a hundred years in London and in Hampshire.

Titchfield 1799-1809

This and two later chapters are based on the files of the now defunct "Hampshire Telegraph". Local newspapers can be a rich mine of historical evidence. Even the advertisements include interesting information. Amongst the sales of property at this time, for instance, we find Meane (Meon) Bye Farm still described as a copyhold estate of 30 acres of arable land with extensive rights of common. A freehold estate at Swanwick was said to abound with much valuable timber for naval purposes, a reminder that ships were still being built which would fight at Trafalgar. A large village property in West Street consisted of two parlours, a kitchen, a washhouse, cellar, a dairy, five bedrooms, a large yard with coach house and stabling for six horses, a woodhouse and other conveniences. The newly-built houses of the gentry were yet more elaborate. Stubbington House had a six stall stable and double coach house with well-placed farm yard, barn, granary, cart-horse stable, and cart lodge, piggery, poultry and pigeon house, a large walled garden, hot and green houses, melon ground, shrubbery, lawn and paddock. Crofton House was described in typically flowery agents' language, "commanding interesting marine views and diversified prospects of the rich surrounding country which abounds with game, the roads good and the neighbourhood select and social with a pleasure ground embellished with full-grown forest trees and plantations, a walled garden in perfection". It had numerous family bedchambers as well as a powdering room, for those who wore wigs, and, even at this early date, water closets.

In 1806 the Coach and Horses changed hands. The inn was described as having for hire single horse chaises, gigs and saddle horses, and neat post chaises "with good horses and careful drivers" at 1s. (5p) per mile. William Glover, who took over the inn, described his advent in typical language of the day:

> "William Glover having lately entered upon the Coach and Horses Inn and fitted it up in a neat and commodious manner begs leave most respectfully to return his grateful thanks to the ladies and gentlemen of the neighbourhood and the public at large for the kind patronage already received and he hopes by an unremitting attention to their commands to merit a continuance of their future favours".

A brewhouse and malt house were sold with the inn which clearly brewed its own beer. Every month an "assembly" was held there. Tickets were between 3s. 6d and 4s. (20p) each - tea included - and dancing began at 8 p.m. A new coach from Gosport to Salisbury carrying four inside and four outside passengers called at the Coach and Horses three times a week, returning on alternate days.

It was the time of the Napoleonic Wars and the local Volunteers were often mentioned. There were 3,700 volunteers in South-East Hants. In 1880 the local volunteers were under the command of Captain and Adjutant Missing, of the well-known local family. At a meeting they "resolved to serve in the defence of their King and Country until His Majesty should dispense with their services". When on one occasion they spent ten days in Southampton the conduct of the officers and men was described as "highly exemplary and meriting the warmest praise of the inhabitants". On another occasion they went to a dinner at Havant at which "the evening was spent with the most refined convivial enjoyment and the bosom of the company was warmed by a flow of the most loyal and constitutional oaths". Because of the fear of French invasion, arrangements had been made to remove infirm persons and cattle from the coast. In September 1805, when the Prince Regent passed through Titchfield, the Volunteers were only given one hour's notice and only some of them could be assembled. However, the Prince still inspected them, and Captain Missing addressed His Royal Highness, saying how happy they were to pay their respects to him. The Volunteers presented arms as the Prince entered and left the town. They seem to have drilled every other Sunday all through the winter. In 1808, then called the Titchfield Volunteer Light Infantry, they were inspected by Lieutenant Colonel Mannock, when they marched in double-quick time and fired blank cartridges with great steadiness and precision.

A cricket match was mentioned at Hook Gate, one of the gates on the Common, between the gentlemen of Titchfield and those of Gosport for 50 guineas. Booths and "a good ordinary" (meal) was provided.

There was a private school called Titchfield Academy run by R. Dodd for "instruction in the several branches of useful literature and a diligent attention to health, morals and improvement". Later he advertised that he instructed his young gentlemen in "the principles of useful science and in the habits of Christian probity". A school "for the reception of young ladies" was also opened, in 1805, by the Misses Danford.

In 1806 there was an advertisement for a Master of the Workhouse. He was expected to be sober, active, and steady, and he was to appoint a Mistress with similar qualities. Persons who could superintend the woollen manufacture would be preferred.

View from the West

Also in 1806 there were a number of robberies in Fareham and Titchfield, and it was thought that the persons concerned had been harboured and allowed to remain in the ale houses. The publicans were told to have people out by ten o'clock in the evening. There was also a local protection racket: a Mr. Jessie Mitchell, described as an Army clothier, received a letter which demanded money; otherwise "not all the power on earth could save him from the Midnight Assassin" to "the great terror and alarm of his family and the manifold injury of public society". One at least of the local thugs could have stepped into a Dickens novel a few years later. John Peermin, wanted for shooting a lamb at Warsash, was described as raw-boned and powerful with a scar on his nose, which was turned to one side. He was reported as having been seen crossing Bursledon Bridge carrying an axe, a gun and a saw.

Another problem of the time was a rabies scare. Two mad dogs had passed through Titchfield and Stubbington and had bitten a great number of cattle. As a result, dogs had to be kept in for three months. People who had been bitten travelled all the way to Southampton, then a spa town, to dip in the local water which was supposed to have curative properties!

The Turnpike

In the Middle Ages the manor was responsible for road maintenance, but with the dissolution of the monasteries and the redistribution of landed estates in Tudor times the duty devolved on the parish. By the Highway Act 1535 each farmer, for every ploughland held, had to provide for four days a year a cart and two men, and every other householder had to put in four days labour. The work was supervised by an unpaid Surveyor of the Highways nominated by the parishioners. As can be imagined this system was inefficient, and roads, especially main roads, were inadequately maintained. As long as most overland goods were carried in sacks or panniers on packhorses, the system was tolerable, but with the increasing use of carts and carriages from the end of the 17th century, local people came to form trusts or companies to be responsible for sections of roads and obtained powers by Act of Parliament to charge for their use. Toll houses were built and gates erected across the roads.

The Titchfield-Cosham Turnpike Trust was formed by an Act dated 1810. It was 7 miles, 2 furlongs, and 186 yards long, and there were six gates and toll bars, and toll houses at Blackbrook, East Cams and Wymering. The Blackbrook toll house was at the corner of the A27 and Gudge Heath Lane. It had a weighing machine, because tolls depended partly on the weight of the vehicle. There were bars across Gudge Heath Lane and Redlands Lane. The East Cams toll house was on the north side of the A27 about fifty yards to the west of the point where it is joined by Down End Road. Wymering toll house was on the old road about 200 yards to the west of Wymering Church. The trustees were local landowners or people holding property. They included Admiral Sir Francis Austen (Jane Austen's brother) who lived at Cosham, Colonel Thomas Hore of Heathfield House, and Major Wingate of Crofton House. The day to day running of the trust was the responsibility of a Clerk, who from 1833-72 was Mr. T.F. Kelsall, a solicitor living in Westbury Manor in Fareham.

As well as repairing roads, Turnpike Trusts also had powers to provide new stretches of road. Until 1811 the road from Fareham to Titchfield went along Catisfield Road, down Fishers Hill to Stony Bridge and then along Mill Lane. It was not until the formation of the trust that the road from Catisfield fork and down Titchfield Hill was built. The estimates for the erection of the bridge across the Meon, dated 1810, are still in existence; the new road was opened on 1 June 1811.

The illustration from Mudie's *Hampshire,* which was published in 1838, shows a wooden fence being erected and was probably engraved not long

The Turnpike about 1815

after the road was completed. The turnpike had a striking effect on the appearance of Titchfield : to allow for its approach direct into East Street, a house was demolished, leaving a narrow gap like a gateway, which formed a dramatic entrance to the village for everyone entering from the east. Some writers in fact have wrongly speculated, mainly on the evidence of the "gateway", that Titchfield might once have been a walled or at least "fortified" town. We can also guess that it was the turnpike which caused the removal of the market hall from the Square, but as well as the effect on its appearance, the road also had an important effect on the village's economy. As long as the main road from Fareham came down to Stony Bridge and Place House, much traffic turned right via Segensworth and thence either to Funtley or to Curbridge and Botley. Now the new turnpike and the recently-built bridge at Bursledon (1799) routed traffic through Titchfield itself and thence via Sarisbury to Bursledon and Southampton. The mid-nineteenth century was to be a period of relative prosperity for the tradesmen and innkeepers of Titchfield. The other turnpike into the parish, the Lower St. Cross, Mill Lane and Park Gate, also of 1810, began the development of the Park Gate area which continues apace in the 1980's.

Road-building and maintenance proved then, as today, to be more expensive than anticipated. In 1815 it was stated that the trust's annual receipts were insufficient to cover liabilities, and in 1818 all expenditure on the road ceased until further ordered. It is no wonder that the Surveyor of the Highways in Titchfield complained about the state of the road.

Milestones were erected in 1815, three of which still exist; part of one is in the wall of the Co-operative premises in West Street, Fareham. There was also one half way down Titchfield Hill, and a boundary stone of the same period still stands by the bridge itself.

Tolls were fixed by Act of Parliament. As they had to be paid at each gate horse travel became expensive. A private carriage (landau, chariot, curricle, barlin, phaeton) had to pay 3d., a stage coach 6d. (2½p), a drove of oxen 5d. per "bore", a wagon according to the width of its wheels .. 6 ins. or upwards 3d., less than 4 ins. 4d., because a wide wheel did less damage to the gravel roads. Later in the century a steam carriage had to pay 2s. (10p) for each wheel.

With the arrival of the railways the income from tolls dropped dramatically, in fact by £12,000 in Hampshire between 1837 and 1850, and so did the amount spent on the roads. From 1877 responsibility for the repair of the roads was transferred to a local Highway Board and the toll houses were either demolished or converted to private houses.

The Brewery and the Inns

Like tanning, brewing was in early times undertaken by many ordinary tenants: the licensing of brewers and the testing of ale was one of the duties of the abbot's court in the Middle Ages. The regulation of brewing and beer retailing continued to be an important function of the court in Elizabethan times: among the offences considered in  one court were "for using the trade of a brewer - whether he be a prentice in that trade we know not"; "for selling beer at the fair - we know not by what measure"; "for selling beer by the stone jug"; "for having a gallon (measure) chained at the stable door"; "for selling wine in quarts not sealed". But the business gradually became concentrated in fewer, more professional hands, and carried out with permanent equipment; the brewery later to be called Fielder's Brewery was founded in Bridge Street in 1741. In the mid-nineteenth century there were three breweries - in Bridge Street, in East Street and in Church Path - and in addition the Bugle did its own brewing. Only Fielder's Brewery survived into recent times. It stood on the south side of Bridge Street west of the canal and the bowling green. As well as the brewery, J.R. Fielder and Sons in their latter years supplied ten public houses in the district - the Brewery Tap, the Queen's Head, the Fisherman's Rest, the Jolly Farmer, the Bold Forester, the Sir Joseph Paxton, the Sun Inn, the Osborne View, the Coal Exchange, and the King's Head (once in Fareham West Street). The smell of the brewery, the sight of Fielder's drays and lorries, and of course the taste of the beer are nostalgic memories for older villagers. The company was sold in 1961, most of the buildings were demolished and a group of private houses built on the site. The attractive brewer's house and some small outbuildings still stand at the west end of the site.

There were taverns in Titchfield in the fourteenth and fifteenth centuries, but the first inns we can actually locate are the George, at the north corner of the Warebridge, and the Inn House in West Street in 1546. An inn called the Nag's Head is mentioned in the late seventeenth century and the Bugle seems to have been the centre of fashionable local life in the late eighteenth and early nineteenth centuries when "assemblies" were held there. By then three more of the existing inns had appeared - the Coach and Horses, the Queen's Head and the Wheatsheaf; in addition there were five inns which have now disappeared - the King's

Fielder's Brewery

Head and the Red House in South Street, the Crown in Mill Street, the Clarendon in East Street and the Horse and Jockey in West Street, making twelve inns altogether at that time. During the turnpike era the provision of food and drink for the coaches and for the carriers' waggons which had regular timetabled stops in Titchfield was an important economic function of the village. The Fisherman's Rest began its existence as a small tannery, and was converted into the Railway Inn when the railway navvies were working at Segensworth in the 1880's, changing to the present name when they moved on.

STOUT

BREWED AND BOTTLED BY
JOHN · R · FIELDER & SON · LTD
THE BREWERY · TITCHFIELD · HANTS
Founded 1744

BROWN

❋ **ALE** ❋

JOHN · R · FIELDER & SON · LTD
THE BREWERY · TITCHFIELD · HANTS

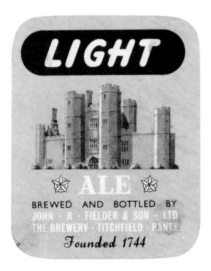

LIGHT

❋ **ALE** ❋

BREWED AND BOTTLED BY
JOHN · R · FIELDER & SON · LTD
THE BREWERY · TITCHFIELD · HANTS
Founded 1744

ABBEY

❋ **ALE** ❋

JOHN · R · FIELDER & SON · LTD
THE BREWERY · TITCHFIELD · HANTS

Some of Titchfield's Ales

The Tannery

Tannery workers

In early times most families prepared hides and skins for domestic use, but professional tanners and leather workers appear in early medieval times, and were certainly at work in Titchfield by 1300. Their pits and workshops seem always to have been sited along the river bank between the corn-mill and the Warebridge, particularly in the area where the stream running under the High Street from Barry's Meadow provided an additional water-supply. This location also had the advantage of allowing the noxious waste to be carried away by the high tides under the Warebridge.

Titchfield market seems for centuries to have been an important local centre for butchers, so there was a regular supply of hides. The ox bones built into a wall in West Street, and those used to form the foundation of a floor in a recently excavated house are striking evidence of this trade. Another necessary item was the oak bark which produced the tannin, and this was for many years collected from the woods, particularly in the north of the parish. An interesting entry in a local school log book shows that even in the late nineteenth century children were reported as absent because they were helping with the bark harvest. The bark was stripped from felled trees in April-May when the sap was rising and then stacked in heaps to dry before being carted to the tannery. The local coppices also provided the faggots - bundles of small branches and twigs - used in heating and drying processes. Lime, another necessary substance, had to be brought to Titchfield, probably in early days by boat.

In the nineteenth century the tannery covered a considerable area, and consisted of numerous sheds and pits. The curing pits were filled with water to which the oak bark, broken into finger-size pieces, was added until the liquid, now called liquor, was of the correct strength. When the hides arrived at the tannery they were dressed, that is stripped of tails and surplus meat - a useful addition to a poor worker's table. The skins were then hung over pits of strong lime water before being transferred to the scraping shed. Here skilled operators stretched the skins over curved boards and removed the hair with sharp scrapers - a delicate operation, for any cuts in the skin marred its quality. The skins were then rinsed in the river, and finally hung over poles in the curing pits. A young skin needed only nine months but that of an old steer as much as eighteen months to complete the curing cycle. During that time, the skins were transferred into stronger and stronger liquor with lime added, then taken out, rinsed again, and dried before the rolling took place. Great care was again necessary to see that the rollers were perfectly clean, to avoid marks on the hide. Most of the finished hides, now known as 'butts', were sold to the trade, but some were used locally, women being employed in making leather boot laces and tags; it is said that at one time Titchfield leather was used for making footballs and football boots in Portsmouth.

Up to 1945 the tannery was dominated by its tall brick chimney, but in the whirlwind which swept over Titchfield one afternoon in October of that year it blew down and was never replaced. Like the gas-holder, the tannery chimney is for older people a memory of a different kind of village from that of today. The tannery, like the brewery, ceased operating only comparatively recently, in 1955 (sold 1961). If older inhabitants have visual memories of those days, they can also recall the smells: when the wind blew from the east the village could be filled with the acrid smell of the tannery, mingling with the smells from the brewery and the gasworks, and in the early mornings those from the four small bakeries which were operating until about 1950 (now only one). In earlier times it is said to have been the practice, in Titchfield and in Fareham, to cover the road outside the homes of sick people with dried, spent tan bark in place of the straw used elsewhere to deaden the sound of passing horses and carts. After the closure of the tannery, the site was for a time occupied by the Sustanum Company. It has now been partially modernized as a small industrial estate, but a number of interesting buildings of the eighteenth and nineteenth centuries still remain.

Tanners were mentioned regularly in the village records from the fourteenth to the nineteenth century. The construction of the canal in 1611 presumably required the resiting of their yards. The site traditionally identified as the wharf at the head of the canal is in fact part of the site of the nineteenth century tannery, and it may be that one function of the canal was intended to be the shipping of tanning materials. There was a tannery building in 1753, and the tithe award map of 1837-8 shows a continuous strip of fellmongers' and tanners' fields along the canal between the Crofton and Fareham roads. Later the central part of this strip was taken for the churchyard extension, and the southern part became merely a garden, still called Skinhouse Piece, leaving the northern part to become the single large tannery of recent times. In 1753 the owner was a Mrs. Moyle; for some time in the nineteenth century the owners were the Munday family; and from about 1890 to 1961 the Watkins family.

Some other buildings in the Village

The true age of a house in Titch-field as elsewhere cannot always be deduced by looking at the frontage, for it was fashionable at certain periods to modernise by adding or removing features, just as we do today. The Bugle Inn is a good example; its front elevation was raised to form a parapet with false windows on the top floor, hiding the old roof line with real dormer windows.

Great Posbrook

The oldest houses in the village are probably those in South Street - Nos. 7 to 13 - where a fourteenth century storehouse, perhaps for the abbey, appears to have been converted to dwellings in the sixteenth century - after the Dissolution; but the first floor floorboards are still oak planks two inches thick, made to support a heavy weight - such as sacks of grain or other heavy stores.

Fifteenth century

There are at least a dozen houses in Titchfield built in the fifteenth century. These were of the hall type, of two or three bays with an open hearth on the floor in the middle of the room, the smoke rising through two storeys to a louvre set on the roof ridge. Evidence for such fires remains today where the roof timbers are still covered with soot. All these houses had inglenook fireplaces inserted in about the sixteenth century, and from that period onwards many alterations and additions were carried out. Now it is the fashion to uncover those old inglenooks and expose the timber framework. Some of the largest fifteenth century houses were roofed with Devon slates, and the humbler dwellings with thatch - both types being given tiled roofs in the eighteenth century. Another feature of fifteenth century buildings was the large sectioned oak timbers; this type can be seen in the West Street houses, Nos. 17 to 21. When houses were thatched they were spaced well apart to lessen the fire risk, but with the change to tiled roofs it was possible to infill simply by building a front and back wall and roofing over. This can also be seen at Nos. 17 to 21 West Street.

Sixteenth century

Examples of sixteenth century houses with their timber frames can be seen in West and South Streets. The framing is slighter and the panels smaller; the present brick infilling between the tarred beams was originally wattle and daub, and a coat of plaster later covered the whole elevation. Mud walls are still found in some of the cottages and many had unglazed windows with bars and shutters.

Seventeenth century

During this century national events, including the Civil War and the Fire of London had their effect on building techniques, and Titchfield itself was in a period of decline. The building of new houses practically halted; only two houses can be found of this period, and alterations to the elevations of two others. In this century brick superseded timber as the main building material and, following the burning of London, new regulations brought a stricter control of building methods. From now on, wood could not be used for external walls but only for windows and doors. A house of this period in upper West Street has its end facing the road and an oak block with the date 1690. The brickwork is in Flemish bond with moulded bricks around the chimney.

Gateway to Old Lodge ————cᵒᵘ

Old Lodge off the footpath at the corner of East Street is also of this period and although it has been somewhat enlarged, it still retains its original east end showing features of classical design with moulded bricks and pilasters. This is a good example of the change brought about when bricks replaced wood: a similar feature may be seen on the east end of No. 11 Church Street.

94

One of the most interesting houses in Titchfield is No. 7 Church Street. It was built in the fifteenth century as a dwelling of three unequal bays - a very large house at that time. It had a central hearth, the soot-covered roof timbers from which are still visible. In the following century two large inglenook and two bedroom fireplaces were inserted. In the seventeenth century the timbered front was replaced by brickwork decorated in Jacobean style strapwork, with diapers in blue bricks below. The windows were still unglazed with shutters to cover the openings at night - the hooks of which can still be seen. One hundred years later Georgian-type sash windows were inserted and fake panels used to cover the old front door, which was made of planks.

The most interesting of the seventeenth century buildings, the Market Hall, has of course disappeared; so too have the stocks, once in front of the Bugle, and the permanent market stalls in the Square.

Eighteenth century

Looking around the Square, one sees no buildings with frontages earlier than the eighteenth century, but if one looks at the rear of some of these buildings it is obvious that some of the cottages sited at right angles to the Square are of a much earlier period. It would seem that sometime in the eighteenth century the Square was enlarged and the little alleyways (called "drokes") were blocked off. At the side of the Bugle is a row of fifteenth century cottages, access being through a narrow arched door from the street. At the side of the chapel behind an eighteenth century front, are more houses of the fifteenth - sixteenth century period. The Independent (Congregational, now Evangelical) Chapel is itself an eighteenth century foundation, from 1789, but the facade was rebuilt in the nineteenth century, and again in the 1970's. Opposite the chapel, nos. 15-19 High Street, Barry's Cottages, are almshouses founded by the Earl of Southampton's Charity.

Perhaps because in the eighteenth century the tenants still maintained certain common rights in the open fields, Titchfield unlike other small towns did not see the building of larger houses with drives and gardens on the edge of the older village. Only one house of this type exists, Guessens on Coach Hill, which takes its name from the old Garston in the corner of which it stands. Instead, the better-off village families devised various ways of improving the ancient tenements. One was to apply a facade and later a parapet facing the street; another was to build a high brick wall on to the street, windowless or with small plain windows, while the main domestic rooms faced a yard or garden at the rear. Buildings of this type can be seen in Mill Street, at the bottom of Coach Hill and elsewhere in the village.

Regency Style

Only one house of this type may be found in the village. It is near the junction of High Street and East Street and stands out among the older houses with its three storeys, semi-circular porch and rendered elevation.

Nineteenth century

Early in the last century, as we have seen, a new front was added to the Bugle Hotel with double bay windows, and the imitation third storey windows merely added for effect. The shops at the corner of West Street and Church Street had bay windows upstairs, so that the shopkeepers (who usually lived over their shops), could have a view up and down the street. At the bottom of Church Street the large vicarage was built in 1851 on the site of an earlier sixteenth century and Queen Anne building. The Parish Room on the corner of High Street and Southampton Hill was built in 1890.

West Street circa 1905

Twentieth century

In the present century very few houses have been built in old Titchfield, but quite a lot of development has taken place, notably on Coach Hill and at the top of West Street. There are also a few new houses on the old Brewery site in Bridge Street and some - Chapelside - partly on the site of the Congregational Chapel schoolroom.

The green space at the bottom of West Street was formerly occupied by a row of old cottages which were removed and rebuilt in Liphook. Halfway up West Street, the open space on the left had thatched cottages on it until about 1950, when they were condemned and had to be pulled down. Fortunately in the past 25 years, the qualities of such cottages have been recognised, and instead of being demolished many have been modernised and extended to become attractive and desirable properties.

Perhaps the most significant change in the appearance of the village in recent years, particularly around the Square, has been the conversion of shops into private houses or offices. Directories from the turn of the century still list a great number of shops and small businesses and many residents can still recall the people and their occupations at a time when the village was a largely self-contained community. It is regrettable that only a handful of these shops survive at the present time, but there are signs that the tide is turning again for shopping in the village.

There are a number of large farms or small manor houses scattered over the parish outside the village, among them Great Funtley Farm, Segensworth House, Crofton Old Manor, Great and Little Posbrook and Brownwich Farm. Two of the ancient farms - Park Farm and Great Abshot - have been converted to modern uses: another, Little Park, is being swallowed up in an industrial estate; and Whiteley Farm, closely associated with the third Earl, is threatened by the next phase of planned development.

Great Funtley

97

Titchfield about 1850

From the middle years of the nineteenth century the number of sources available to us for the history of the village greatly increases. From 1801 the Census returns give us regular information about the population of the parish; the successive editions of the Ordnance Survey maps provide more and more detailed information about the location of buildings; the Tithe Award of 1837-8, by which the ancient system of tithes was replaced by cash payments, resulted in the compilation of a detailed survey and map; printed Directories from time to time summarised activities in the parish; the files of local newspapers became richer in content; and so on. A great deal of information from this period remains to be summarised and analysed, and we do not pretend in this present volume to have done more than dip into it.

Although the population of the parish continued to increase (to 3,957 in 1851) it was not increasing at the same rate as in the late eighteenth century, and certainly not as fast as in neighbouring Fareham, Gosport and Portsmouth, which were benefiting in those years from the coming of the railway and from naval and military activities. Titchfield became something of a backwater, though still a fairly prosperous one. There was no railway station in the parish and in spite of the turnpikes, road transport was still very slow, so that the increased population continued to do most of their shopping in the village. A plan of the village centre at this time, based on the Tithe Award and the Census returns shows the great variety of shops, trades and occupations at a period when there were few mass-produced consumer goods and no chain stores: there were around the Square three drapers and tailors, three boot and shoemakers, two butchers, two bakers, two grocers, and so on. The market was still held in the Square (our only picture of the market in operation dates from this period), but it was becoming less a farmers' market with livestock sales, and more a retail market for fruit, milk and vegetables. In fact, the character of local farming itself was changing: the old sheep and corn husbandry was being replaced by mixed farming and horticulture and more and more of the village fields are described as occupied by market gardeners rather than by farmers.

Within the small industries and trades of the village we can see beginning the process which economists call "horizontal integration", the gradual merging of numbers of family businesses into one or two larger concerns. There were three small breweries, for instance, in the mid-nineteenth century, and by the end there was one; there were several tanners and fellmongers, by the end only one. It is a process which has continued until recent times.

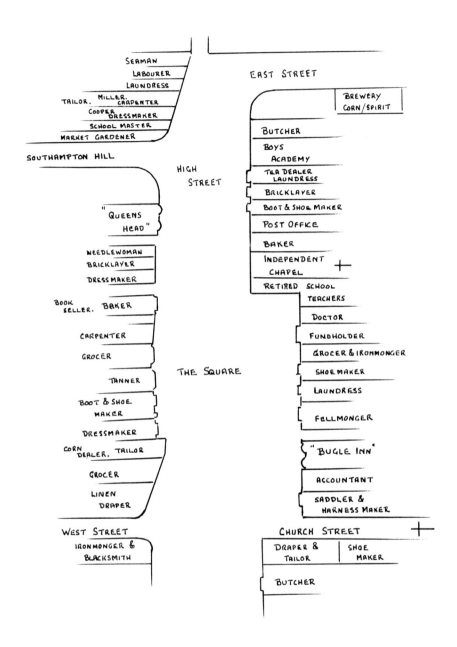

SEAMAN
LABOURER
LAUNDRESS
TAILOR. MILLER. CARPENTER
COOPER DRESSMAKER
SCHOOL MASTER
MARKET GARDENER

EAST STREET

BREWERY CORN/SPIRIT

BUTCHER

BOYS ACADEMY

TEA DEALER LAUNDRESS

BRICKLAYER

BOOT & SHOE MAKER

POST OFFICE

BAKER

INDEPENDENT CHAPEL

RETIRED SCHOOL TEACHERS

DOCTOR

FUNDHOLDER

GROCER & IRONMONGER

SHOE MAKER

LAUNDRESS

FELLMONGER

"BUGLE INN"

ACCOUNTANT

SADDLER & HARNESS MAKER

SOUTHAMPTON HILL

HIGH STREET

"QUEENS HEAD"

NEEDLEWOMAN
BRICKLAYER
DRESSMAKER

BOOK SELLER. BAKER

CARPENTER

GROCER

TANNER

BOOT & SHOE MAKER

DRESSMAKER

CORN DEALER. TAILOR

GROCER

LINEN DRAPER

THE SQUARE

WEST STREET

IRONMONGER & BLACKSMITH

CHURCH STREET

DRAPER & TAILOR | SHOE MAKER

BUTCHER

People who lived around the Square about 1840

99

Brick and tile making, in early times undertaken on small sites throughout the parish wherever suitable clay was obtainable, became concentrated in the large works at Swanwick and Funtley. The ancient salt-making industry, older than the Romans, finally succumbed to cheap salt from Cheshire, and charcoal making to coal brought in by coastal shipping. An even older activity - fishing and the collection of shell fish along the coast - flourished for a time with the growth of population, until the pollution of the Solent reduced the catches.

Over the ancient parish as a whole, we can see in the 1840's and 1850's the process of creeping suburban development beginning. On the western edge of the parish along the line of the turnpike and around Sarisbury Green were spreading more and more stuccoed gentlemen's residences and neat brick villas, whose occupants looked not to Titchfield for their occupations and their shopping, but towards Southampton and Woolston; on the eastern edge in Catisfield, Crofton and Stubbington similar houses looked towards Fareham, Gosport and Portsmouth. It was yet another process which went on until recent times and which almost destroyed the lively village community of shopkeepers and tradesmen of the nineteenth century.

The Titchfield Gasworks

Aerial view showing Gasometer

Newcomers to the village will be surprised to learn that Titchfield was the proud possessor until 1951 of a gas works - with a prominent gasholder - in its early years the envy of the surrounding communities!

The Titchfield Gas Consumers Company Limited was formed in 1865 with a share capital of £1,500 in £5 shares "for the purposes of lighting the Town of Titchfield and the neighbourhood thereof with gas". The 1867 Post Office Directory confirms that the streets were lit with gas, though Kelly's Directory of 1899 still states that they were lit by oil! The original works were in Bridge Street and the entrance can still be seen; just inside this street at its western end and on the north side is a house which has in its driveway the weighbridge over which the ingoing coal carts proceeded into the works via a narrow passageway.

Little is known of the early years of the company except that it was operated by a lessee who also leased two other works at Emsworth and Petersfield. The Titchfield works was one of the earliest to adopt tar firing of retort house furnaces. In 1908, the undertaking was incorporated under the Companies Consolidated Act and its name became the Titchfield and District Lighting Company Limited. However, the company passed through difficult times, and like many small companies at the time fell into the hands of the mortgagees who in 1910 sold the £5 shares at 2s. 6d (12½p) each to a Mr. F. Bunney, the miller in Mill Street. Later in that year he sold the company for £1,200. The new owners raised additional capital of £4,800, put the undertaking on a sound basis and bought more land next to the existing works and running through to Frog Lane (now Castle Street). A new works was built consisting of 11 retorts and a two-lift gasholder of 30,000 cu. ft., together with the usual condensers, washers and purifiers.

Under the Titchfield District Gas Act 1913 the area of supply was extended to the parishes of Sarisbury and Hook-with-Warsash. The Act was opposed by the Gosport Gas and Coke Company, who had had powers to supply parts of these parishes for the previous 48 years, but had never done so. Strangely, Sarisbury and Hook had previously refused permission for mains to be laid in this area but reversed their decision when the Act was passed.

By 1915 the annual output was five million cu. ft. of gas - five times more than in 1909. There is a note showing that public lighting in Titchfield then consisted of 34 gas lamps and the company was also supplying Catisfield, Swanwick and Park Gate. In 1933 the area of supply was again extended, this time to include Bursledon, and in the following year a new 50,000 cu. ft. holder was commissioned.

In 1939 consideration was given to buying bulk supplies from Southampton via a pipeline over Bursledon Bridge but terms could not be agreed. The gradually increasing use of electricity at the time made gas less profitable, particularly where coal had to be brought by road and in 1943 the undertaking was offered for sale though neither Portsmouth nor Southampton would accept it.

However, after the 1948 Gas Act and the nationalisation of the industry, Titchfield was connected to the local gas grid and like many others this small works closed. The final year saw the production of 18 million cu. ft. of gas. The gates were finally shut on 11 October 1951, and the gasholder, once as firmly a part of the village scene as the Market Hall had been, was demolished.

Schools

John Leland, the traveller, mentioned the grammar school near Stony Bridge in 1542, and we can guess that it had been set up by Thomas Wriothesley to replace the education which the abbey had provided for a small number of boys. Although the school continued to be marked on maps for two hundred years, we at present know absolutely nothing about its history or who might have attended it; and thereafter we know little about any schools in Titchfield until a Parliamentary Report of 1818 on the "Education of the Poor". This tells us of the existence of a number of fee-paying schools; a school for young ladies, one for young gentlemen, and ten other 'petty' schools which in all provided for 227 children, though another 70, mainly children who worked on weekdays, attended the two Sunday Schools. Small private day schools continued to exist throughout the nineteenth century and most of the better-off parents seem to have sent their children to these, but the poorer people could not: the report says that the poor persons of the area would have liked their children to be educated but in fact they were having to earn their living at a very early age.

It was in an attempt to meet the needs of poorer people that in 1830 the National School was built in West Street, at a cost of £400. It was enlarged in 1855 and again in 1871 (this time at a cost of £200). "National" schools were built with financial help from the Church of England and, as shown by the log books, the local vicar and curate spent several hours at the school each week (the School Log Books from 1873 to 1901 are in the County Record Office). A teaching system by monitors (older boys and girls) operated for most of the nineteenth century, and we hear only of a single master for the boys and mistress for the girls - indeed the grant would not have supported more staff.

Local trade directories record that in 1899 the School catered for 344 children with an average attendance of 290. For the first time a teacher for the infants is mentioned. The numbers attending school reflect the fact that families were large at that time. In 1891 a penny a week was charged for each pupil, and stories are told by the older residents of some poor families sending their children to school on a rota system because they could not afford to send them all at the same time - even if this meant breaking the attendance requirement which was by then statutory.

At the turn of the century school hours were from 9 a.m. to 4 p.m. with a 45 minute break for lunch. At that time there were three or four teachers in addition to the Heads of the three departments but the former were

Old National School, West Street

qualified only by experience (or inexperience!) receiving their training before or after school from their department Head. The school was all-age, young people leaving to go out to work.

In 1933 the National School was closed. Infants and Juniors henceforth attended the County Primary School built by the side of the new by-pass of that time. Secondary pupils were in future to go to the Sarisbury Senior School, now Brookfield School; a small number were given scholarships to attend Price's School in Fareham or other local schools. For a short time the retired headmaster's family ran a small private school in the National School buildings, but in the Second World War it was requisitioned and used as a military headquarters. After the War it was for a time derelict, but in 1953 Meon Cross Boys Preparatory School was founded there. Later this moved to Catisfield, where it still flourishes, and the old National School building now houses an antique business. The building is an interesting reminder of nineteenth century educational architecture and the recollection of the old school in its heyday arouses nostalgic memories in many of the village's older inhabitants.

West Hill Park

West Hill Lodge was built about
1770 by the third Peter Delmé, as
his family's pied-à-terre in Titchfield on the final abandonment of
Place House. In that romantic age
he fancifully thought of it as a
hunting lodge, though the extent
of hunting possible in the decayed
strip of woodland beside the old
Hunt Pond was very very modest

West Hill Park

by the standards of his Wriothesley predecessors! Peter's premature death
and the family's financial difficulties meant that the Delmé's themselves
never lived in the house after this period. Instead it was occupied by a
succession of other families. In 1803 the tenant was Lord Henry Paulet,
Vice Admiral and Lord of the Admiralty; in 1834 it was William Hans
Sloane Stanley, a descendent of the better known Sir Hans Sloane: it was
Stanley who built the North Wing. In the middle of the century the house
was occupied by members of the Baring family: the painting over the
chancel arch in the parish church was the gift of the Marchioness of Bath in
memory of her sisters, the Hon. Misses Baring of West Hill. Other tenants
were T.W. Hornby, Montague Foster, Lady Louisa Fielding and James
Dredge, a distinguished civil engineer who interested himself at West Hill
by planting many of the fine trees which still stand in the grounds. The last
private occupier was Lord Frederick Hotham, from 1907 to 1919: his two
surviving daughters Lady Clitheroe and the Hon. Jocelyn Hotham both
remember standing on the balcony at West Hill watching the Titanic sail
down the Solent on its ill-fated maiden voyage. In those prosperous
Edwardian days the old Hunt Pond was dug out again and a "Chinese"
bridge built, which was hung with oil fired lanterns for summer evening
parties.

In July 1919 Charles Ransome bought the house and in January 1920
opened it as a boy's preparatory school. In the sale particulars the house
was described as "a spacious and elegantly built lodge and approached by a
long carriage drive through a small parkland. It commands extensive and
delightful views of the Isle of Wight, Spithead and Southampton Water,
contrasted by the picturesque beauties of the New Forest. The grounds are
adorned with many fine cedar, yew, specimen conifers shading wide spread
lawns, flower-beds and borders". There were many outbuildings, a stable
block (now classrooms), a farmery, kitchen and box gardens; behind there
was a large six acre strawberry field, from which much of the fruit was sent
to Covent Garden.

Play the Game, Chaps!

In the Delmé and Paulet days there was a small ballroom where in the evening there were two large mirrors that were let down into the cellars during the day to reveal two windows behind. This former ballroom and the drawing-room now comprise the school library. The circular drawing-room communicated with the conservatory, which still retains its magnificent tiled floor. The principal staircase is of stone and semi-circular in shape, and has a richly inlaid mahogany handrail. Half-way up the flight is the entrance to the North Wing - this contained the original billiard room with carved oak panelling and an Organ Gallery which sadly no longer exists today. The first floor held the principal bedrooms and a spacious library fitted with a carved oak mantel and antique Persian tiles. The rooms had access to a balcony overlooking open country, the Solent and the Isle of Wight. The North Wing was connected into the main structure of the house in 1930.

West Hill School has existed as a successful enterprise since 1920. A number of extensions and adaptations have been skilfully made to the original buildings, and the fine parkland is still largely intact. The school was evacuated to Cornwall during the Second World War, when the house was used as a military nursing hostel, and part of the grounds as an R.A.F. sports field.

Titchfield 1875-1894

The last decades of the nineteenth century saw the end of Titchfield as an administrative unit of some importance. The "manor" was by now little more than an antiquarian survival; the old functions of the civil parish were gradually being transferred to more modern authorities and, as described earlier, the ancient ecclesiastical parish was broken up as the population increased. For a time Titchfield had a parish council: now it is no more than an electoral ward and a fairly small ecclesiastical parish.

We can trace the signs of change in the "Hampshire Telegraph". We hear for instance of the end of the turnpike: in June 1878 it was proposed that the turnpike gates and bars should be removed. Tolls had ceased to be collected in that year and in October the toll houses were sold by auction.

The prices of houses advertised for sale are ridiculously low by modern standards: three cottages in Church Street were sold for £95 and a house in the High Street for £215. A house of six rooms with four acres of market garden land brought in an annual rent of £40 and a shop and house in the High Street, of ten rooms with a carpenter's shop and stable, was let for £19 11s.

That age was dominated by the horse as ours has become by the car. Many houses had stables and coach or cart houses, and we hear mention of broughams (closed carriages), pony phaetons and (at a sale of the contents of the Bugle) a landau (open carriage), two waggonettes, a dog cart, a horse dealer's "skeleton" brake, four serviceable horses - and 20 fat pigs!

Farms too were still dependent on the horse. At Little Abshot Farm in 1886 seven cart horses were sold as well as five double-thill (shaft) shallow-bed waggons and four dung carts. As well as horses, a variety of other livestock was still kept: at Segensworth Farm 60 pigs, 22 geese, 10 turkeys and 60 poultry were sold, and at Westhill Farm 144 Sussex ewes.

The newspaper continued to report meetings of the manor courts. On the death of Mr. H.P. Delmé, the new Lord of the Manor Seymour Robert Delmé held Courts Baron for the Manors of Titchfield, Segensworth, Crofton, Newland and Cams at which were presented the deaths of copyholders. The parish meetings in the vestry were still being held, and surveyors of the highways and overseers of the poor appointed.

Though changing, the village was still a very lively and active community. One of the most flourishing of local societies was the Ancient Order of

Foresters whose "court house" was then at the Coach and Horses. In 1888 they held a procession headed by the band of the 3rd Volunteer Battalion, Hampshire Regiment. The brethren were in regalia on horseback and on foot, carrying the banners and flags of the order. They paraded in the town and visited the houses of the principal inhabitants. After a dinner for a hundred people they adjourned to the meadow at the foot of Hollam Hill where there were swings, "shooting saloons", sports and dancing. There was also a Choral Association which provided concerts - at one of which they sang a mass by Mozart followed by popular songs such as "Foresters, sound the joyful hour" and "Sing, birdie, sing". An Oddfellows Lodge was opened in 1878; this had a juvenile branch which on one occasion had an outing by wagon to Gosport, and across the ferry to Southsea. There was also an Independent Order of Good Templars who met in a Temperance Hall in South Street. There was a Band of Hope connected with the Titchfield Congregational School and a branch of the Conservative Primrose League.

The kind of entertainment provided at such events was typical of its period. Singing was very popular and the song titles very sentimental such as "Silver Moonlight", "Come, like a beautiful dream", "Dream faces" and "A night with a baby". Other mysterious entertainments mentioned are a "pedestal skate dance", a comic sketch, an "exhibition of dissolving views" and the "embodiment of an Ethiopian Serenader", said to be very popular.

Harvest dinners were mentioned, which were often combined with cricket matches and dancing. We also hear of dancing on the green, running for prizes of print dresses and stockings and, of course, climbing the greasy pole. On another occasion there was an exhibition with a magic lantern given to the Congregational Sunday School, the comic pictures provoking "loud bursts of merriment". On that occasion a Christmas tree 8 ft high (covered with sweets and other presents) was produced from behind a curtain.

A working men's club and coffee room was started next to the Bugle in 1882, to keep working men out of the pub (so we are told), at which tea or coffee was 1d a cup and games and a bagatelle board were provided. In the same year a Temperance Reading and Coffee Room was opened on the corner of High Street and East Street. A flower and industrial show was held at West Hill Park, "to stimulate and encourage the cultivation of flowers and vegetables among artisans and cottagers". A treat for the "aged poor" was held in 1894 - for those over 55! The room was decorated with mottoes and evergreens and blazing fires gave the room a cosy appearance. There were readings, recitations and music, and the aged poor were given a bun, an orange and an illustrated picture card.

Carnival Day about 1890

Harvest thanksgiving services were regularly reported, but in 1879 the reporter was unusually blunt and critical. The alms, he said, were collected in bags by gentlemen in long cassocks and very short surplices, which had a somewhat queer appearance on bulky bearded men. There were four hymns besides an anthem and other "choral effusions", and he thought the beautiful simplicity of the service was marred by this "superabundance" of music. He was impressed, (or amused), at the "reverential rising up of some half a dozen females when the choir and clergy entered the church". There was "something irresistibly ludicrous in seeing the same parties make such a bend of genuflection when the Gloria was sung as almost to disappear from the vision of the expectant congregation". A procession at the beginning and end of the service contained no sense at all, he thought. It began with a young chorister carrying a banner very like a fire screen, "with some device which I could not make out but which, on enquiry, I was told was generally supposed to be a likeness of the Vicar! I am sorry to say from the broad grin which now and then illumined the face of the banner bearer that he did not seem much impressed with the dignity or solemnity of his office".

Plymouth Brethren opened a chapel in South Street in 1882, and in December they held a public baptism in the canal, near the bridge in Bridge Street. A large number of people were gathered to witness the strange sight, and some of them were said to be rather free in their denunciation of what they considered to be a mockery.

We hear of some field sports. In 1881 a party of gentlemen from the New Forest, with a pack of hounds, worked the river up to Wickham. In the following year four otters were caught, one of them being an old dog otter weighing 28 lbs. In 1883 Mr. Walter Long's pack of hounds had a day's outing at Titchfield. You will remember that otter hunting had also been popular in John Missing's day.

Truancy from school was even then a problem. In 1879, a report of the school board for Titchfield and Rowner said that 744 places were required in the schools, but when an inspection was carried out there were only 544 present. One girl only attended 37 out of a possible 279 times! Parents were prosecuted and various excuses were produced. One family of nine had only 13 shillings a week to live on. Two children were sent home because they only came with 2d when they should have produced 3d (education was not yet free). They could be sent home because of dirt and vermin. This we were told would seriously interfere with the comfort of the rest of the children. One boy at the Titchfield National School stole the dinners of two of his fellow scholars: he was sentenced to 24 hours confinement in the police station and 9 strokes with a birch rod.

Drunkenness seems also to have been a problem and resulted in various forms of violence. One man used a knife at the Wheatsheaf and was given a month's hard labour. For brandishing a stick and bad language another had to pay 5 shillings and 8s. 6d costs. An Irish woman, a hawker of fancy goods, was fined 10s. (50p) for breaking a pane of glass. One drunk, a negro, who had gathered a mob around him and was using disgusting language, refused to walk away and was conveyed in a wheelbarrow to the police station in Fareham!

Poaching was often reported. One man was fined for an activity which went back to prehistoric times - using a net and eel spear near Crofton House. Two men were fined 10s. or 7 days' hard labour for setting traps and using guns (they protested that they had only caught a mouse!). Trespassing for game and conies (rabbits) and using a ferret cost a 20s. fine (£1). Various kinds of theft are noted. A "traveller" stole a blanket and was given two months' hard labour; a girl of 13 was given 21 days and four years in an industrial school for stealing a shawl worth 4s; a boy stole 24 strawberries worth a penny and was given 24 hours imprisonment and was to be fed only on bread and water.

None of these offences seems to be very serious, but in November 1891 a most horrible murder was committed in West Street. A Mr. and Mrs. Hinton had moved from Chichester into a small, old-fashioned cottage there. Mr. Hinton was a collar maker and obtained work at the shop of one Muckett, a harness maker, but lost his job and picked up a precarious living from the sale of winkles gathered along the beach. His wife sold flowers. Their three children, said to have been starved, were turned out into the streets in bitter weather at all hours of the night and left to depend on the charity of neighbours. During one week they had only boiled bran to eat. Then one night the neighbours heard loud screams and cries for help from the Hinton's house. Mrs. Hinton had killed two of her children and wounded the other, then attempted to commit suicide. She was taken to Knowle Hospital, the nearby hospital for the mentally-ill. This story is sadly reminiscent of that in Thomas Hardy's novel "Jude the Obscure".

Titchfield in Victorian and Edwardian times, in fact, had a reputation as a "rough" village. This reputation was partly derived from its old markets and fairs: farmers from outlying hamlets used to come into the village to do business, then drink in the pubs until their horses led them - asleep in their carts - home again; the gypsies, too, trotting their horses up and down the Square and arguing flamboyantly, added a distinctive flavour to the place; so did servicemen on leave from barracks and ships in Gosport, Portsmouth and elsewhere. At the same time, the declining status of the old town seems to have induced here a kind of touchy pride: there were

The Afternoon Call

fierce rivalries with nearby towns, particularly with Fareham and Wickham. Football matches (as long as the football club existed) were ferociously contested. The young men of Titchfield and Fareham had a treaty: Titchfield boys going beyond the old railway arch at Fareham station could expect trouble; so too could Fareham boys coming over the crest of the hill at Ranvilles Lane: in between was a no-mans-land. Old-fashioned policing by the local bobby and old-fashioned caning in the local schools had little impact on these historic activities. Something of the tradition still lingers on even in our own more civil times: it is perhaps no accident that Titchfield Boxing Club has a notable record of success!

A Song from Titchfield

"Buttercup Joe" was commonly heard in Titchfield pubs fifty years ago. Towards closing time one of the older men, in a fair state of inebriation, would rise shakily to his feet and deliver one of several versions of this song, the verses normally more bawdy than those printed below! But the singers particularly relished the chorus, which they sang slowly, plaintively and with great feeling, miming the movements of ploughing and milking, and ending in a posture of sly, defiant humility while holding an imaginary buttercup. It is possible that two earlier songs - a rumbustious bawdy song and a melancholy chant - had at some time been welded together. The song was 'collected' by a folk-song enthusiast at the beginning of this century at Itchen Abbas near Winchester, but the reference to Fareham, so well calculated to provoke an audience response in Titchfield, and the song's popularity here, suggests a local origin. Unexpectedly, villagers who attended Titchfield school in the 1920's remember being taught a respectable version of the song there. It is said to have been sung long before, in one of Garrick's London pantomimes, in the eighteenth century, perhaps by an unknown Hampshire man who attained some celebrity in the metropolis. There is still some fascinating research to be done about the song, but here it is:

Buttercup Joe

I am a jolly sort of chap
My father comes from Fareham
My mother's got some more like I
and knows well how to rear 'em
Oh some they call I "Bacon Face"
and others "Turnip Head"
But I can prove that I'm no flat
Although I'm country bred.

For I can guide a plough or milk a cow
Or I can reap or sow
(I'm) as fresh as a daisy (as lives) in the field
(And) they calls I "Buttercup Joe".

Those nobby swells they laugh and chaff
To see I eat fat bacon
They could not touch that country stuff
But that's where they're mistaken.
On wine and grog they do their airs
And lord it at their ease
But I give I fat pork from the sty
Or a lump of bread and cheese

For I can guide a plough etc...

Oh bain't it prime in Summertime
When we go out hay'making
The lasses they will all turn out
And freedom will be taken
They like to get us country chaps -
Of course, in harmless play -
They like to get us country chaps
And roll us in the hay.

For I can guide a plough etc...

You should just see my young woman
They calls her our Mary
She works as busy as a bee
In Farmer Kellyson's dairy
Oh bain't her suet dumplings good
By Jove I mean to try 'em
And ask her if she wouldn't splice
With a rusty chap like I am

For I can guide a plough or milk a cow
Or I can reap or sow
(I'm) as fresh as a daisy (as lives) in the field
(And) they calls I "Buttercup Joe".

Titchfield 1897-1932

George V Coronation Celebrations

From the files of the "Hampshire Telegraph" for this period we get a picture of a community undergoing first slow and then steadily accelerating change.

At first, we seem still to be in a traditional society. The manorial court, for example, was still in existence: in 1897 the "general Courts Baron of Lt. Col. Emilius Charles Delmé Radcliffe and George Delmé Murray Esq" were held at the Bugle. The local gentry continued to enjoy a P.G. Wodehouse style of life: in 1905 West Hill Park was described as having "14 bedrooms, a bath, a spacious hall, four reception rooms, a conservatory, a grand billiard room with an organ gallery, a noble loggia and verandah, complete offices, stabling for seven, delightful old pleasure grounds, ornamental stream and lake, sumptuously fitted electric light and good water". Down in the village, still without piped water or sewerage, properties were let at what now seem ridiculously low rents. Three cottages in Frog Lane were let for between 2s. 4d and 2s. 9d (12-13p) per week; East House in East Street with four bedrooms and three reception rooms, for £28 a year; and what were described as "extensive business premises" - a large shop with a dwelling house in the centre of the village - were let for £50 a year.

The furnishings of these houses, too, tell of a bygone age. Furniture sold at Crofton included brass bedsteads, feather beds, brass fenders. Hip baths, sponge and foot baths were sold at St. Margaret's, and at another sale in the village, a music "canterbury" and stool, a davenport, ottomans, a three-tier whatnot, a sutherland table and a donkey bath chair. Horses were, at first, the main form of local transport: one sale included a rally cart, a landau painted black with red lamps and patent brake complete, a waggonette, a governess cart, and a tip cart with "raves" (rails).

But the year 1920 saw some ominous changes. The sale of one contractor's stock seems to mark the passing of the horse: a brake to carry 18, a two pair omnibus, a landau, three horse-drawn vans, a bay gelding of 17 hands and various sets of harness. In that same year there were complaints about steam engines stopping at the bottom of Fareham Hill to take water from the river, though prohibited from doing so; and the Parish Council - like a latter-day King Canute - asked the County Council to impose a speed limit of 5 m.p.h. in the village. In fact by the end of the decade, the village had its first by-pass, on the line of the A27 past the mill.

The early 1920's saw other necessary changes. In 1919 the village houses still obtained their own water: some used wells; others had their own pumps; some carried buckets from the flight of steps at the edge of the canal in Bridge Street; some from the stream in Timbers Mead above Barry's Meadow; others from the village pump at the corner of East Street and Southampton Hill; and many from the famous donkey drawn "waterworks". But in 1922 and 1923 water-mains were provided, to which most houses were connected by the end of 1923. The flushing of sewage into the river Meon was making the river and canal increasingly polluted: so in 1923 the Parish Council agreed on a sewerage scheme, which was largely completed in 1925. In 1923, too, electric light was switched on for the first time.

Through all the changes the lively social life of the village continued unabated. The Bonfire Boys Society continued to be active. In 1919 the Society held a peace demonstration, and in 1925 there were two bands in the procession, a four horse stage coach, Mr. St. John the baker's trade car - a huge loaf, a car for the Titchfield Gas Co., and a van for Messrs. J.H. Fielder and Sons, brewers.

In the same year there were peace celebrations in the village at West Hill Park (lent by Lord and Lady Hotham), when tea was provided for the children and old people. There were sports, a maypole and songs. Later in the year there was a dinner in the Drill Hall for those who had served in the Forces.

Titchfield Waterworks

A choral society met in the Drill Hall and the Fire Brigade held a concert there. There was a Men's Social Club which met at the Queen's Head, a Football Club and a Titchfield and District Horticultural and Fanciers Society. At a strawberry show held in 1923 there were 158 entries. There was also a Constitutional Association. An annual fair was held at Hollam House, "by kind permission of Miss Agnes Hewitt"; in 1923 it lasted two days, being opened on the first day by H.R.H. Princess Beatrice and on the second day by Lady Davidson. In September 1922, the Friendly Societies - the Buffaloes, the Foresters and the Odd-fellows - held a spectacular parade: the procession was led by the Congregational Brass Band and the banner of the Botley Society, followed by members of the various societies marching in full regalia.

The Bowling Club was an innovation: "Bowling Club formed. 29 January 1923. The Chairman of the meeting was Mr. W.T. Freemantle. It was resolved to form the club and the offer of land from Mr. J.H.H. Fielder was accepted. The club was to be called the Titchfield and District Bowling Club". £20 towards the cost of laying the green was promised by local gentlemen. "…1st June 1923. The green of the Titchfield Bowling Club was opened on Monday evening by Col. The Hon. C. Brabazon, and afterwards a match between members of the home club and the Fareham Bowling Club was played, the result being a win for Titchfield by one

117

point. After the match the visitors were entertained at the Queen's Head by the home bowlers, when an enjoyable time was spent. A capital selection of music provided by the Titchfield Brass Band, under the direction of Mr. Westall''.

Of the many village notables of those years, perhaps the most active was A.E. Mason, who kept the chemist's shop in the Square. He was treasurer of the Bonfire Boys in 1911, and secretary of the Cricket Club in 1913 (when he took 105 wickets in one season). In 1923 he was re-elected as People's Warden, was Chairman of the Horticultural and Fanciers Association and was Chairman of the Parish Council. The extinction of the parish council when Fareham Urban District was created in 1932 marked the sad end of a long era of energetic local government.

Titchfield celebrates

Titchfield Schooldays:
memories from the 1920's

We moved to Ranvilles Lane (then known as Love Lane by the locals), Catisfield, in 1923. The only other house in the road then was Hollam Lodge, occupied by a Colonel Collier, who moved from there in about 1928 to Somerset and was later killed in a hunting accident. I was six years old when I started in the Titchfield School - which held all the boys and girls up to the age of fourteen. If one lived (as I had previously lived) more than three miles from a school, one need not start until the age of  six. An unqualified teacher, Miss Carden, taught the younger infants and a Miss Richards the older ones. In the boys' department standards one and two were taught by a Mr. Toombs, Miss Rogers took two and three while the headmaster, Mr. Upshall, took standards five, six and seven.

The roads everywhere were untarred and as no boys then wore long trousers, falls sometimes produced nasty cuts to knees as well as hands. The playground also was rough and along the bottom bordering Barry's Meadow was a low spiked iron fence. I remember a girl impaling her leg on the fence while attempting to get a ball from the meadow.

Games for the boys were conkers (in the season), then hoops - an old bicycle wheel rim made the best one - marbles and tops. I have whipped a top all the way from the school up to my home in Ranvilles Lane. Luckily there was not much traffic about! The most frequent vehicles were the Foden and Sentinel steam wagons which had solid tyres. They were used for carting gravel from the pits at Warsash to all the building sites in the neighbourhood. With no by-pass until 1929 all the Portsmouth-Southampton traffic passed through Titchfield. The sharp bend at the bottom of Southampton Hill was improved in the twenties by demolishing three cottages.

All the farmers used horses; even the fire engine was drawn by two of them. There were three blacksmiths' forges in the village; the last (in West Street) closed after the Second World War. Cart horses on the road needed new shoes every month - and cost 50p per set. I remember a wagon

119

loaded with corn in sacks and drawn by two horses trying to get up Fareham Hill and slipping to their knees on the icy road. Of all the children then at school I was the only one whose father owned a car and sometimes, if it was raining, my father met me at school, and as many of the Catisfield boys as could get in had a lift. The car was a bull-nosed Morris Cowley.

The only treat we ever had at school was an occasional Punch and Judy show.

George Powell in East Street ran a carrier service. Each day one van went to Portsmouth and another went to Southampton. His son, Reg Powell had a charabanc and ran a service to Fareham on Saturdays. Otherwise, people walked! We used to walk to Hill Head for a bathe.

The Town Crier then was 'Knocker' Taylor, who lived in Church Path - then known as Winkle Alley, or 'the Alley'. Another character living there was 'Admiral' Munday, to whom many comical sayings were attributed, as, for example, "The first ladder I went up was down a well"! There were seven bakers in the village: White, Knight and Read in West Street; Waters and Powell in South Street; Lankester & Crook in the Square and Couzens in East Street. They were mostly one-man businesses and it was a tough life in winter to leave a hot baking oven to go out and deliver the bread in a pony trap.

Discipline at Titchfield School was strict. Even a misdemeanour committed by a boy going to and from school could result in a caning. Other offences like talking in class could also get a stroke of the cane on the hand. At age twelve I left Titchfield School and began to take a bus to Fareham (costing a penny) to attend Price's School. The by-pass road was then being constructed. Welsh miners were employed for this work; they ran small trucks on rails down the hill and then tipped the soil which had been dug from the higher part of the hill by a Ruston Bucyrus digger. The advent of the by-pass and the beginning of the bus service affected local traders, and two businesses closed in East Street. It is a process which has unfortunately continued until quite recently.

(Chris Draper)

The Bonfire Boys

It is possible that the Titchfield Bonfire Boys took over a tradition of riotous celebrations which may have been originally connected with the defunct autumn fair. There does not appear to be any first hand documentary evidence for the foundation of the Bonfire Boys. In 1888, the local paper says the Society had been founded some years before, when a tar barrel was burnt in the Square, "but things got so hot that the police interfered". In 1919 another tar barrel was burnt in the Square and there were complaints that the paintwork of the houses was damaged and the fireworks damaged someone's curtains. In 1898, the red banner of the Society is mentioned, bearing the inscription: "Titchfield Bonfire Boys, established 1880", and in 1907 it said that the Society was founded 25 years before. The first meeting mentioned in the Hampshire Telegraph was in 1887, at the Temperance Hall, to decide on the date of the demonstration.

There does not appear to be a real description until 1894, when members in costume paraded round the town with a guy and rocket stand on a trolley. In the evening they were accompanied by the Titchfield Drum and Fife Band and torch bearers to a paddock belonging to Mr. Wilkins of the Bugle, where there was a "pretty display of fireworks". Three years later the display seems to have grown because there were 150 people in the procession and a bonfire 20ft high and 40ft round in "Bells Field", Coach Hill, with fireworks. In 1898, however, there were some interesting tableaux: "The last stand of General Gordon in 1884" escorted by a guard of lancers in white helmets; the Khalifa was burnt in effigy. There was a trades' procession - the cars of the tanners engaged in fleshing and tanning hides, blacksmiths' cars, butchers, bakers etc. At this time the Oddfellows and Foresters always had tableaux in the procession. In 1902, there were decorated cars and two bands, one being the Titchfield Mounted Band.

The account given in 1907 is so delightful in its quaint Victorian style that it is worth quoting in full. From it one can gather that many ideas now used by the Society, such as giving money to charity and the rhymes which appeared at the bottom of posters from 1946-61, were then in use. One great difference was that in 1907 most, if not all, of the tableaux were horse drawn.

> *"All Titchfield was on its feet on Monday night the august occasion being the November carnival and torchlight procession in memory of the misguided Guido Fawkes. Collections were made for the hospital and the unsuspecting were greatly trapped by this formula: "Gie us a penny, sir. It is the greatest night of the year". Truly Titchfield rose to*

The Cause of Many Troubles

the occasion. The carnival Committee turned its frolicsome pen to facetious bill composition which announced in fat type that the demonstration would be held on Monday November 5th W A D S (work all day Sunday) that it would be a 'sumptuous O K show'; that the procession would be 'preponderous' (shades of Dr. Johnson preserve us!): that the mounted police would be under the command of Sergeant Buzfuzz and that a 'conglomeration would be unearthed'. The rest of the bill was descriptive of the line of the route and local witticisms were indulged in exclusively: objects of interest on the itinerary such as Jones' shop, Smith's backyard and Robinson's trade being alluded to in a way that was unfortunately caviare to the general. Monday's affair divides into two sections. In the afternoon the procession went round the town in the full light of day and satisfied the closest inspection. In the evening torchlights, Roman candles and lanterns lent glory and imagination to the scene, greatly hid defects and furthered the fun of the fair. For a village effort the carnival was a marvel of completeness and good organisation and was worth going a long way to see. Portsmouth had not yet managed better cars or devices and Titchfield seems to have much more of that humour that makes the world go hum. A couple of old bicycles that ought to be in the South Kensington Museum, so quaint were their frames, were ridden by the tired tramp tourists; the fire Brigade was caricatured with a red barrel on wheels with a manual hose; a living skeleton, a Mephistopheles, a barbaric barber, women and wine and the gaming table with its consequent caged convict breaking stones, and an airship "Polly Secundus" cleverly rigged up on a bicycle and illuminated with acetylene lamps. Then the Foresters and Oddfellows with their usual tableau cars as to the value of provision against sickness, Jack was to be seen saying farewell to the Miller's daughter with the wheel going round and round and dripping real water, a car illustrating the sad story of the 'Mistletoe Bough', fish frying, blacksmithing and various trade cars including bun making. The cars were decorated with material and foliage and at night lighted with Chinese lanterns, while followers carried oil flares casting a lurid light on niggers and grandees, cowboys and swashbucklers, old hags and bearded patriarchs. Masks were much worn doubtless because in a village where everyone knows everyone else (often their business as well), it is a great occasion to be able for a little while to sink one's own identity. The small boys fairly throbbed with excitement. Lights burned and crackers banged off around your feet and over your head and so great was the crush that Titchfield could hardly move through its own streets, which it meagerly lights with oil, made all the more impoverished-looking by the generosity of Monday's private illuminations. Music was supplied by the Bishops Waltham Brass Band and the Titchfield Fifes and Drums which took part in the procession through the streets to the recreation field and Messrs. A.E. Mason, T. Conway (Chairman of the Committee) and C. Kingsman marshalled the procession, the Secretary being Mr. E. Bowers and the Assistant Secretary, Mr. Freemantle. There was no organised fire display but the fun of a Bal Masqué was kept up until a late hour long after the last torch had spluttered out. Then Titchfield went home through streets dark with wet mist and redolent of benzolene and gunpowder smoke".

The astonishing growth of the Carnival can be seen in the accounts. In 1929, the balance was £65 3s. 10d and in 1976, £5,473. The Society ceased to operate in the two World Wars and in 1914 £3 was sent to the Royal Portsmouth Hospital, leaving a balance of £1 14s. 7d. In 1929, £1 15s. was paid for a pianist and stringed instruments. These, apparently, were used at the smoking concerts which were held in turn at each pub to make money for the Carnival. A fee of 9s. (45p) was also given to the 'Street Crier'. The Town Crier wore a cocked hat, breeches and stockings and carried a bell (three people who were Town Criers were Bill "Spudgell" Burgess, Jim Bowman and "Knocker" Taylor).

In 1946, after the Second World War, the Society was revived in celebration of the return of Servicemen from overseas; it is said that during the war, on the day when the Carnival would have been held, someone walked round the streets beating a drum, and from that time the Carnival has become steadily bigger. Some of the Bands have been very distinguished: the Black Watch, the Greenjackets, the Duke of Edinburgh's Gurkha Rifles, the U.S. 3rd Air force, H.M.S. Daedalus, the Royal Hussars and the Royal Marines. On one occasion, (1976), there were 11 bands and two companies of Majorettes.

The tradition of providing tableaux has been well maintained. Over the years there have been many topical ones: Mount Everest being climbed, King Farouk gambling - with Suez as a stake, Journey into Space, Teddy Boys, the Beatles, Chi-Chi and An-An, Buzby. Many of the tableaux show considerable ingenuity and are beautifully made. There has been a great variety of set pieces: the English Rose Garden, Quality Street, Madame Tussaud's, a fairy grotto, Swan Lake Ballet, Hear my Song, Violetta, the Cresta Run, Rhapsody in Blue, Alice in Wonderland, Snow White and the Seven Dwarfs.

Tableaux, of course, are only part of the procession. There have been scarecrows on horseback flanked by Arab outriders, gypsies and witches, children as animals and toy soldiers and in many other kinds of fancy dress, the Bonfire Queen's throne drawn by four horses and flanked by postillions and outriders, pram races, shire horses pulling a brewery dray, traps, broughams, wagonettes (Florence Nightingale was shown riding in one of these), drunks and beatniks, giants on stilts (one got on his stilts from the balcony above what was Collihole's Shop), Can Can dancers, balloons, girls from St. Trinians, tribal warriors, characters from "Oklahoma", Mr. Marples' Dream Car - which fell apart -, Lady Chatterley and the Gamekeeper and almost anything else you could think of.

The centre piece of the day is the crowning of the Bonfire Queen in the Square. Then there are the thunderflashes, crackers, a man putting out his burning trousers, "the milling, cheering, singing, cracker-tossing crowds". After the procession there is the bonfire, fireworks, funfair and the magnificently decorated shops, houses, pubs and hotels to be seen. "Bonfire Day" is the day in the year when Titchfield reminds the towns and villages around that it is still a really lively community.

124

Titchfield from the air

Customs and Superstitions

Although Titchfield is an ancient and historic place it has few of the odd customs and superstitions which we find elsewhere in the countryside. There are, it is true, a number of ghost stories: spectres dressed in white at the abbey; hooded ghosts at St. Margaret's; the drowned Dutchman in the

Child's shoe found at 7 Church Street

river; a ghastly tanyard worker immersed in his own liquor; a funeral procession which walks for ever across the fields from Brownwich; the murdered soldiers at Three Stone Bottom. But these are stories, not customs. It is possible that some of the older practices, like the mummers, became absorbed in the Bonfire Boys procession and so lost their distinctive character. If the bonfire celebrations themselves had ancient origins we do not know what these were. Of course older people conventionally touch wood, avoid crossing knives and so forth, but we can only quote two distinctive customs. We learn of one from the diarist Pepys: as he rode past Crofton Church he was told that the graveyard there was sown with sage. The other was the custom of building a shoe into the fabric of newly erected buildings: an example can be seen in the Bugle, and others have been found during recent renovations in Church Street, South Street and elsewhere.

Titchfield has of course had a long and close relationship with orthodox religious practices through the parish church, the abbey and the chapel; and it has also been for centuries a market town frequented by strangers with new ideas. Perhaps these two influences have between them wiped out the rustic pagan practices which persisted elsewhere. But a courteous inquirer with a tape-recorder might still recover some ancient tales from older people, particularly from the more distant farms.

The Strawberry Industry

It is a pleasant historical curiosity that after four centuries of being allowed to remain as common grazing land, while the people of the parish got on with more productive activities elsewhere, Titchfield Common should for more than a century after its enclosure have become one of the best known features of the district, recognised by people to whom the abbey, the church or the Earls of Southampton meant very little. "Hampshire strawberries", most of them grown between the Meon and the Hamble, became - and in spite of some contraction in acreage, still remain - a valued commodity in the fruit markets of most of the major cities of the kingdom.

Until the late 18th century, the agriculture of the parish continued to be dominated by two traditional staple commodities - grain and sheep - with the addition of root crops in rotation, but with the growth of Portsmouth and Gosport, and the improvement of communications, first by the turnpikes and then by the railway via Botley through Fareham to Gosport in 1841, the farmers of the parish began to turn their attention increasingly to the supply of fresh fruit and vegetables to the growing towns and the Navy. Mudie remarked in 1839 that "the climate is favourable for the growth of vegetables" and later in the century the parish was said, with some exaggeration, to supply most of the cabbages to the Royal Navy. Strawberries as a commercial crop are said to have been introduced into

Off to Market

the district by the Carpenter-Garnier family of Rookesbury Park near Wickham, who in the 1800's encouraged the tenants on their smallholdings at Hundred Acres to undertake their cultivation.

Certainly by the time the enclosure of Titchfield Common was complete, the market for strawberries was sufficiently well developed to make it an attractive crop for the new smallholder tenants there to grow. Strawberries need little capital investment, produce income from a crop in the first year of cultivation and can be easily propagated by "runners". The problems of disease which became evident in the 1930's and 1940's were absent on the fresh soils of the common in the 1860's. Given buoyant markets, a smallholding of two or three acres, worked by members of a single family and with low overheads, could produce a good annual income.

In the heyday of the industry it was easy to obtain credit from local tradesmen: "pay you in the picking" was the jocular phrase. A family with four, five or six acres could become relatively wealthy, able in a few years to build one of the characteristic red-brick villas of the period by the side of the corrugated iron shed which had until then stored their tools and baskets. Cheap seasonal labour for the "bedding-down" (with straw) and the picking was provided by the gypsy families who normally arrived in the parish in their horse-drawn caravans in the early summer (traditionally on Wickham Fair Day, May 21st), and left again to find odd jobs near the seaside towns in July and August.

The thin, stony soils of much of the old common, useless for the ploughland agriculture of earlier times, was exactly suited to the shallow rooted strawberry plants. Where they lay over gravel, the soils were well-drained and warmed quickly in spring sunshine, and the warm prevailing wind coming over the waters of the Solent and the Hamble reduced the risk of frosts in the critical weeks of flowering. Little heavy equipment was needed: ploughs, harrows and horse-hoes could when necessary be hired from those farmers who still practised traditional mixed farming. Many strawberry growers had a single pony for carting the crop daily to the market or the railway station, but others relied on neighbours with larger two-horse carts who acted as carriers for the rest.

In the 1860's and 1870's horse-drawn carts had to leave Titchfield and Locks Heath at 2.30 a.m. to reach the markets in Portsmouth and Southampton; others went to the nearest railway stations at Botley and Fareham. The jam factory which was built near the Sir Joseph Paxton Inn in the 1880's made little difference to these transport problems, for only the inferior end-of-season fruit was sold for jam-making. It was the construction of the new railway and the opening of the station at Swanwick in 1888 which transformed the local industry and produced something like a gold-rush or an oil-strike. Special strawberry trains left Swanwick every evening during the season, to reach particularly the Covent Garden market early next morning, but also Birmingham, Manchester, Glasgow and other cities. The roads into Swanwick Station were sometimes at a standstill with long queues of horsedrawn carts waiting to unload. Up to 100,000 baskets of strawberries could be loaded at Swanwick Station alone in a single day; over 3,000 tons of strawberries passed through Swanwick in the 1913 season. In the late 19th century steam-driven traction engines were also introduced to draw heavy loads to the stations and markets, and later with the introduction of the petrol engine, motor vans and lorries were rapidly adapted with special racks for the same purpose.

From the beginning Hampshire had been in competition with Kent for the London strawberry market. Much depended on the vagaries of the weather - cold winds over Kent might give Hampshire a critical fortnight's advantage in getting the highly-priced early strawberries on to the market, but a warm Kent spring might lead to a sudden fall in prices just as the Hampshire season was getting into its stride. By the First World War the local industry was also meeting competition from imported French strawberries and, as communications improved, Belgian and Dutch, even Mediterranean, strawberries added to the competition. The use of glass cloches and other forms of frost protection, though widely used by local growers, also enabled growers further north, for example in the Vale of Evesham, to become more competitive. The strawberry bubble began to burst in the inter-war period. The economic depression of those years, the competition, and the development of crop diseases resulted in a steady reduction in acreage. After the Second World War, higher wages for agricultural workers, and then greatly increased competition from straw-berries flown in from all parts of the world, accelerated the process. The slaphappy smallholder of the earlier era, living on tick and enjoying his outing to Goodwood Racecourse after the picking, became an anachron-ism. Some expertise, knowledge of plant varieties, artificial fertilisers, insecticides and the like came to be essential. But the Hampshire strawberry survived, and indeed still survives, with a high reputation for quality and appearance, to find a place at Buckingham Palace garden parties and London's best hotels. Its main competitor in the 1980's is not Kent or Israel or California, but the bricks and mortar and tarmac which are now spreading remorselessly over a Common which in one era produced 3,000 sheep and in another 3,000 tons of fruit. A good, full history of strawberry growing in this area still needs to be written.

Titchfield Fete Baby Show 1921

Titchfield Fire Brigade 1939

Titchfield and War

Titchfield has been fortunate in never (to our knowledge) having been the scene of major conflict: but being on the south coast and near invasion and embarkation points, it has been closely involved in war at second-hand. Henry V stayed at the Abbey both before and after the Battle of Agincourt; the youthful third Earl strengthened the defences, perhaps including St. Margaret's, against the Spaniards; in 1694 the parish register records the death of "an Irishman, a soldier that died at the Nag's Head".

During the early years of the Civil War, Titchfield was for a time seriously involved, lying in a no-mans-land between the parliamentary forces, which were generally in control of Portsmouth, Southampton and other coastal towns, and the royalists, who were stronger in central Hampshire. The fourth Earl, a moderate royalist, and his family, normally followed the King's court around the country, while his elderly mother lived on at Place House; the young Countess was on one occasion given a pass by Parliament to bring her children to Titchfield to see their grandmother. In October 1644 the parliamentary troops assembled at Titchfield (we can guess on the Common) before their abortive attack on Andover. In January 1645 the royalist General Goring, after threatening Portsmouth, plundered the area between Gosport and the New Forest, taking men for the army, horses, cattle, sheep and pigs: it may have been this destruction which began Titchfield's economic decline at that time. King Charles was, of course, taken into custody by Colonel Hammond at Place House in 1647.

Unveiling the War Memorial, Titchfield

First Aid Post 1941

In the Napoleonic Wars the local Volunteers were very active in Titchfield, as later in the nineteenth century were the Territorials. A Drill Hall was built in Mill Street, which in its later rebuilt form has become the Community Centre. In the First World War, older villagers remember long columns of troops marching through the village, and large groups of troops were sometimes billeted in village houses: the house called Mayburys in the High Street was used for a time as a hospital. Like many other English villages, Titchfield lost many young men in both wars, as the Rolls of Honour in the church testify. The Second World War saw much local activity. In 1939 an R.A.F. camp was built on what is now the Plessey site as a depot for the barrage balloons from Portsmouth and Southampton. The coast was fortified against invasion and a gun emplacement constructed at Brownwich; "pill-boxes" were built all over the parish; there was a First Aid post at the Parish Room and a Home Guard unit at the Drill Hall. Later in the war there was an anti-aircraft site at Meon.

In the village itself, British, American and Free French troops were billeted at various times; the best known of these units was No. 12 Commando (later 3 and 9) under the command of Lord Lovat. The old National School in West Street was throughout the war used as a military headquarters. The small B.B.C. radio station in Ranvilles Lane also had an important function: politicians, officers and reporters returning from France through Gosport were able to make their first broadcasts from here. Titchfield has always been closely connected with the Royal Navy and with the Fleet Air Arm: many salty yarns have been, and continue to be, told in its pubs!

Collecting Cockles on Meon Beach

Church Restoration

The Welfare Trust

The Titchfield Welfare Trust was formed in 1969 from the amalgamation, by arrangement with the Charity Commissioners, of five separate charities. The oldest of these was the charity established in the will of the third Earl of Southampton dated 1620; the others were Robert Godfrey's Charity (1897), William Godfrey's Charity (1703), Charlotte Hornby's Charity (1890) and Seymour Delmé's Charity (1894). These charities had as their objects the relief of poverty; assistance to the old; and the apprenticeship of poor persons. The charities owned a number of properties in the village, including Barry's Cottages in High Street, which are let at nominal rents to older villagers. The present secure finances of the trust result from a fortunate transaction of 1861. In that year a piece of charity land was sold for the extension of the churchyard, and the income from the sale was used to buy a piece of land on the newly enclosed common. This land has in turn recently been sold to the County Council and others at a considerably enhanced value.

In the amalgamation of 1969 the newly constituted trust was given the object of "the relief of need, hardship and distress" wherever aid was not available from official sources, and a welcome initiative of the trust has been the conversion of No. 24 The Square to form a well equipped facility for older people of the village, to be known as The Earl of Southampton's Day Rooms (1982).

The opening of the Earl of Southampton's Day Rooms

The Nature Reserve

The area to the south of Titchfield village following the River Meon and the canal seaward is known as Titchfield Haven. The seaward end of this estuary comprises 215 acres of natural marshland, and is of outstanding importance to many species of migrating birds both in summer and winter.

In 1972 Hampshire County Council acquired the land from Colonel J.S. Alston with the intention of creating a Nature Reserve. Colonel Alston had previously himself conducted walks through the area for birdwatchers during the migration seasons. From 1972, when a Warden was appointed, until 1976 when it was officially opened to visitors, much work was done planning, surveying, draining and digging two lagoons. Hides were built, paths laid, and the whole area fenced to protect the Reserve from trespass. Two-thirds of the area are grazed by cattle, both to keep the grass short for wintering wildfowl and to provide some income for the Reserve.

The canal and its sluices make it relatively easy to control the water level over the whole area, which can be varied to form marshes or dry land to suit the differing needs of the birds. The adjacent beaches and mudflats of the Solent contribute to ensuring a plentiful supply of food for waders.

The Titchfield Haven Nature Reserve is now a valuable and successful venture, both as a link in the chain of roosting and feeding sites in the Solent for most types of birds, and as a buffer against over-development in the area. It gives interest and enjoyment to birdwatchers, naturalists, walkers and to the general public. A similar area is to be developed further along the coast to the west. Together with Titchfield Abbey and other historic buildings now open to the public, facilities such as these are ways in which the ancient parish is responding to modern demands. Visitors to the Haven can explore not only the Nature Reserve but also the remains of the seventeenth century canal and (at low tide) the prehistoric site of Rainbow Bar. Intending visitors to the Nature Reserve should contact: The Ranger, Haven Cottage, Hill Head, Fareham (Tel: Stubbington 2145) between 0830 hours and 1630 hours. The Reserve is open from 1st September to 25th March.

Titchfield Today

We have followed life in Titchfield and have watched it develop and change with the times from prehistory to the present day. Titchfield today is a large village full of energy, some people enthusiastically accepting change, others sturdily resisting it. Of course it has its share of the difficulties which beset any community, its share of broken marriages, parking problems, vandalism, graffiti and the like, but it also has an exceptionally fine community spirit. The characteristics of the village, perhaps particularly noticed by those outside it and by those who go away and return, are vitality and enthusiasm, fierce independence yet great friendliness, generated by people of all ages and occupations and contributing towards making Titchfield a very enjoyable village in which to live or work.

Our essential needs can still be provided by village shops, which may have diminished in number, but are in more attractive surroundings and offer a more old fashioned, personal service than large concrete shopping centres several inconvenient and expensive miles from home. We are also lucky enough to have our own village policeman, still to have a village primary school, a fire station, a community centre, a well equipped new surgery, day rooms for the elderly and several excellent pubs.

The two largest employers in the village are the Plessey Company and the Census Office. There are also a number of small businesses, old and new, including over a dozen now housed in the recently redeveloped tannery site. Agriculture, mainly market gardening, still plays an important role here, and local farmers have taken a lead in the flourishing 'Pick Your Own' movement, now a great summer attraction.

On the social side there is a great variety of activity for those who want to join in; the thriving Community Association alone has over twenty affiliated organisations, and the Parish Church and the schools add their contributions to a full village life. All these things need our constant support, for they are worth nourishing. We must also cherish and protect for the future our beautiful old buildings, the meadows and the Haven, for these are irreplaceable assets in a changing world.

Happily the village of Titchfield was designated as a conservation area in 1969 and both before and since that date county and district planning policies have successfully protected Titchfield and the river valley from the flood of suburban development which has spread westwards from Portsmouth and eastwards from Southampton. In the early 1980's a new

Christmas Lunch at the Old Peoples' Day Centre

138

A New Generation

tide of houses and factories was spreading over the western parts of the old Place House Park and over much of the former common. With continued care in planning and development, Titchfield can be expected to benefit from this growth, by providing facilities and services for a rising population. It may not be too fanciful to envisage this historic village playing the same role in a wilderness of brick and tarmac in the 1980's that the ancient church played in a wilderness of marshland and forest in the year 680.

Titchfield Chimneys

Further Reading

Readers intending to walk around the village should buy the *Titchfield Village Walk* leaflet (Titchfield Village Trust). Visitors to the parish church and the abbey can obtain guide books at both places. An interest in the buildings can be followed up through *Hampshire and the Isle of Wight*, N. Pevsner and D. Lloyd (Penguin, 1967). Archaeologists should read *The Archaeology of Hampshire*, ed. S. Shennan and R. Schadla Hall (Hampshire Field Club, 1981), and industrial archaeologists *Hampshire Industrial Archaeology* and *Water and Wind Mills in Hampshire* (Southampton University Industrial Archaeology Group, 1975 and 1978). Good reference libraries will contain the five volumes of the *Victoria County History* for Hampshire (1900 onwards), now out-of-date in some details but still a mine of information. Several valuable articles on the history of Titchfield can be found in the annual volumes of the *Proceedings* of the Hampshire Field Club (1895 onwards), and others in the occasional volumes of *Fareham Past and Present* (1965 onwards). B. Carpenter Turner's *A History of Hampshire* (Phillimore, second edn. 1978) is a popular history of the county as a whole; it can be followed up in *The Small Towns of Hampshire*, M. Hughes (Hampshire Archaeological Committee, 1976) and *Hampshire's Heritage,* ed. M. Jagger (Hampshire County Council 1979). The history of the Premonstratensians is told in *The White Canons in England*, H. Colvin (Oxford, 1951) and that of the Wriothesleys both in *Shakespeare's Southampton*, A.L. Rowse (Macmillan, 1965) and *Shakespeare and the Earl of Southampton*, G. Akrigg (H. Hamilton, 1968). As well as the present volume, the Titchfield History Society publishes a regular newsletter which can be bought by the general public and has several more volumes in preparation.

The Square

Acknowledgements

The committee of the Titchfield History Society would like to thank all those who have helped to make the production of this book possible. We are indebted to those who have contributed to the text or lent illustrations and especially to Vernon Belding for the many beautiful drawings he has done for us. We would like particularly to thank our constantly good humoured and tolerant editor, George Watts, not only for his own articles, but also for making such an excellent whole out of the vast jigsaw of contributions with which he was initially confronted. Special thanks are due to Terry Greene, who cheerfully and indefatigably typed and re-typed the various drafts of the book and to Sally Wise, who spent many hours skilfully co-ordinating in a myriad of ways the entire project with devotion and charm.

We would also like to acknowledge with gratitude the help given in a variety of ways by I.B.M. (UK) Ltd., the Hampshire County Council, Fareham Borough Council, Polygraphic Ltd., the Titchfield Jubilee Trust and many individual members of the Society.

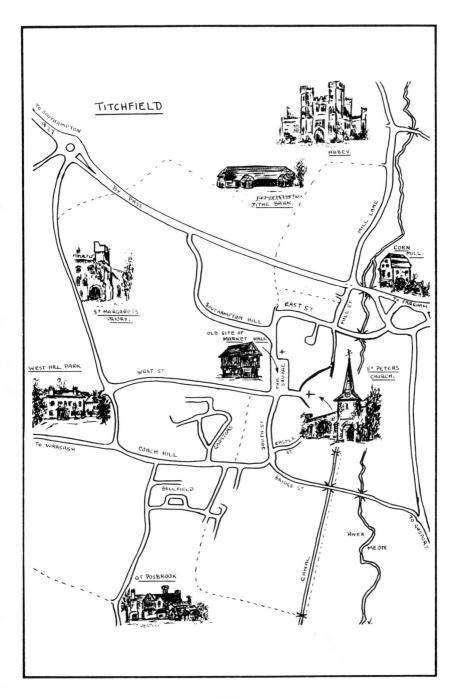

TITCHFIELD

TO SOUTHAMPTON A27

BY PASS

ABBEY.

TITHE BARN.

MILL LANE

CORN MILL.

ST MARGARETS PRIORY.

SOUTHAMPTON HILL

EAST ST

MILL ST

TO FAREHAM

OLD SITE OF MARKET HALL

WEST HILL PARK

WEST ST

THE SQUARE

ST PETERS CHURCH.

GARSTONS

SOUTH ST

CASTLE ST

TO WARSASH

COACH HILL

BELLFIELD

BRIDGE ST

TO GOSPORT

RIVER MEON

CANAL

GT POSBROOK

143